New York State, George James Bayles

Civil Church Law

New York

New York State, George James Bayles

Civil Church Law
New York

ISBN/EAN: 9783337262303

Printed in Europe, USA, Canada, Australia, Japan

Cover: Foto ©Suzi / pixelio.de

More available books at **www.hansebooks.com**

EDITED BY

GEORGE JAMES BAYLES, PH.D.

LECTURER IN

THE CIVIL ASPECTS OF ECCLESIASTICAL ORGANIZATION

COLUMBIA UNIVERSITY

NEW YORK

JAMES POTT & CO.

FOURTH AVENUE AND 22^D STREET

NEW YORK

1898

TABLE OF CONTENTS.

EDITORIAL NOTE.

The Constitutional Guaranties, p. 1.
Grant of Corporate Powers, p. 1.
Definitions, p. 2.

INCORPORATION OF CHURCHES.

Notice of Meeting for Incorporation, p. 3.
The Meeting for Incorporation, p. 3.
The Certificate of Incorporation, p. 5.
Filing and Recording Certificate, p. 5.
Time, Place, and Notice of Corporate Meetings, p. 5.
Organization and Conduct of Corporate Meetings; Qualification of Voters Thereat, p. 6.
Changing Date of Annual Corporate Meetings, p. 7.
Changing Number of Trustees, p. 8.
Meetings of Trustees, p. 8.
Creation and Filling of Vacancies Among Trustees of Such Churches, p. 9.
Control of Trustees by Corporate Meetings of Such Churches, p. 9.
Consolidation of Incorporated Churches, p. 9.
To Maintain Homes for Their Aged Poor, p. 11.
Corporations for Organizing and Maintaining Mission Churches and Sunday-schools, p. 11.
Corporations with Governing Power Over Churches, p. 12.
For the Dissolution of Religious Societies, Except in the City and County of New York, p. 13.
Application of this Chapter to Churches Incorporated Prior to January First, 1828, p. 14.
Application of this Chapter to Churches Created by Special Laws, p. 15.

CHURCH TRUSTEES.

General Powers and Duties of Trustees of Religious Corporations, p. 16.

Table of Contents.

CHURCH PROPERTY.

Limitations Upon Property and Income of Religious Corporations. Inheritance Tax Not Applicable, p. 19.

Property of Unincorporated Society Transferred by Its Incorporation. p. 19.

Correction and Confirmation of Conveyances to Religious Corporations, p. 20.

Judicial Investigation of Amount of Property of Religious Corporations, p. 21.

Acquisition of Property by Religious Corporations for Branch Institutions, Establishment, Maintenance, and Management Thereof, p. 22.

Acquisition of Property by Two or More Religious Corporations for a Common Parsonage, p. 23.

Acquisition of Property by Religious Corporations for Cemetery Purposes; Management Thereof, p. 23.

Sale, Mortgage, and Lease of Real Property of Religious Corporations, p. 24.

Property of Extinct Churches, p. 25.

Mortmain Restrictions, p. 25.

Places in Which Traffic in Liquor Shall Not Be Permitted, p. 26.

Exemption from Taxation, p. 26.

BAPTIST CHURCHES.

Notice of Meeting for Incorporation, p. 29.

The Meeting for Incorporation, p. 29.

The Certificate of Incorporation, p. 30.

Time, Place, and Notice of Corporate Meetings, p. 31.

Organization and Conduct of Corporate Meetings; Qualifications of Voters Thereat, p. 31.

Changing Date of Annual Corporate Meetings. p. 32.

Changing Number of Trustees, p. 32.

Meetings of Trustees, p. 33.

The Creation and Filling of Vacancies Among Trustees of Such Churches, p. 33.

Property of Extinct Baptist Churches, p. 33.

Baptist Missionary Convention, p. 34.

Free Baptist Churches, p. 36.

Table of Contents.

CONGREGATIONAL CHURCHES.

Notice of Meeting for Incorporation, p. 38.
The Meeting for Incorporation, p. 38.
The Certificate of Incorporation, p. 39.
Time, Place, and Notice of Corporate Meetings, p. 40.
Organization and Conduct of Corporate Meetings; Quali-
fication of Voters, p. 40.
Changing Date of Annual Corporate Meetings, p. 41.
Changing the Number of Trustees, p. 41.
Meetings of Trustees, p. 42.
The Creation and Filling of Vacancies Among Trustees
of Such Churches, p. 42.
Limitation of Powers of Trustees, p. 42.
Election and Salary of Ministers, p. 43.
Transfer of Property to Other Corporations, p. 43.

EVANGELICAL LUTHERAN CHURCHES.

Decision by Lutheran Churches as to System of Incorporation and Government, p. 45.

FREE CHURCHES.

How Incorporated, p. 47.
Powers, Limitations Upon Property, Liability of Trustees,
p. 47.
Vacancies in Boards, p. 48.
Pews to Be Free, p. 48.

METHODIST EPISCOPAL CHURCHES.

Corporations for Acquiring Parsonages for Presiding
Elders and Camp-Meeting Grounds, p. 49.

PROTESTANT EPISCOPAL CHURCHES.

The Meeting for Incorporation, p. 52.
The Certificate of Incorporation, p. 53.
Corporate Trustees, Vestry, Powers, and Duties Thereof,
p. 54.
Annual Elections of Incorporated Protestant Episcopal
Parishes, p. 55.
Changing the Number of Vestrymen of Protestant Epis-
copal Parishes Hereafter Incorporated, p. 57.

Table of Contents.

Changing Date of Annual Election, Number and Term of Office of Church Wardens in Protestant Episcopal Churches Heretofore Incorporated, p. 58.

Changing the Qualification of Voters and the Qualifications of Wardens and Vestrymen, p. 59.

REFORMED DUTCH, PRESBYTERIAN, REFORMED PRESBYTERIAN, AND EVANGELICAL LUTHERAN CHURCHES.

Decision by Lutheran and Presbyterian Churches as to the System of Incorporation and Government, p. 60.

Incorporation of Reformed Dutch, Presbyterian, Reformed Presbyterian, and Evangelical Lutheran Churches Under this Article, p. 61.

Evangelical Lutheran and Presbyterian Churches, Changing System of Electing Trustees, p. 62.

ROMAN CATHOLIC AND GREEK CHURCHES.

Incorporation of Roman Catholic and Greek Churches, p. 65.

Government of Incorporated Roman Catholic and Greek Churches, p. 65.

SHAKERS AND FRIENDS.

Trusts for Shakers and Friends, p. 67.

Conveyance of Trust Property of Friends, p. 68.

UNION CHURCHES.

Incorporation of a Union Church, p. 69.

Government of Incorporated Union Churches, p. 70.

UNITED BRETHREN IN CHRIST.

Trustees of a Church in Connection with the United Brethren in Christ, p. 72.

Note.—Under the general title of Civil Church Law it is purposed to edit a series of digests presenting the statute law affecting religious organizations as it is being developed in the American commonwealths.

Such law is not now easily accessible to the great body of church people, yet with the rapid development of church as one of the great institutions of American society there is more and more use for it. Again, the time has passed when even the chief features of the civil church law of all the commonwealths could with convenience be presented in a single volume, and those bearing church responsibilities generally need to know only the law directly defining their duties and rights.

American statute legislation relating to ecclesiastical organization is developing rapidly. It is evident that we are in the midst of a general movement for the broader introduction of purely ecclesiastical elements into the civil law, creating not indeed a civil establishment of religion, but more and more of a legal establishment of church.

In order to set forth this body of law as it develops, in the form best adapted to serve the interests of the whole body of church people, the plan of a series of State digests has been adopted. The type for these digests will be kept standing, and the changes in the law of each State will be presented annually. To extend the benefit of this watch on legislation for churches to the churches themselves it has been arranged that subscribers to any State digest shall receive free of charge for a period of three years after their subscription copy of all further legislation affecting religious organizations. If, however, a general revision of the law should be effected during such a period, the editor reserves the right to bring out another edition.

The general arrangement of the law will probably be the same for each digest: the constitutional guaranties of religious liberty, the general provisions for the incorporation of religious organizations and their regulation after incorporation, the powers and duties of church trustees, and the special provisions for particular denominations. This arrangement will not always follow the sequence of the statutes.

CONSTITUTIONAL GUARANTIES, CORPORATE POWERS, DEFINITIONS.

The Constitutional Guaranties.—The free exercise and enjoyment of religious profession and worship, without discrimination or preference, shall forever be allowed in this State to all mankind; and no person shall be rendered incompetent to be a witness on account of his opinions on matters of religious belief; but the liberty of conscience hereby secured shall not be so construed as to excuse acts of licentiousness, or justify practices inconsistent with the peace and safety of this State.— § 3, Art. 1, State Constitution.

Corporations may be formed under general laws; but shall not be created by special act, except for municipal purposes, and in cases where, in the judgment of the legislature, the objects of the corporation cannot be obtained under general laws. All general laws and special acts passed pursuant to this section may be altered from time to time or repealed.—Art. VIII.

Neither the credit nor the money of the State shall be given, or loaned to, or in aid of, any association, corporation, or private undertaking.—Art. IX.

Grant of Corporate powers.—Every corporation as such has power, though not specified in the law under which it is incorporated:

1. To have succession for the period specified in its certificate of incorporation or by-law, and perpetually when no period is specified.

2. To have a common seal, and alter the same at pleasure.

3. To acquire by grant, gift, purchase, devise, or bequest, to hold and to dispose of such property as the purposes of the corporation shall require, subject to such limitations as may be prescribed by law.

4. To appoint such officers and agents as its business shall require, and to fix their compensation, and

5. To make by-laws, not inconsistent with any existing law, for the management of its property, the regula-

tion of its affairs, ...   and the
calling of meetings of its members.

.   .   .   .

By-laws duly adopted at a meeting of the members of
the corporation shall control the action of its directors.
—Chap. 687, Laws 1892.

Definitions.—A religious corporation is a corporation
created for religious purposes.

An incorporated church is a religious corporation
created to enable its members to meet for divine worship
or other religious observances.

An unincorporated church is a congregation, society,
or other assemblage of persons who are accustomed to
statedly meet for divine worship or other religious observances, without having been incorporated for that purpose.

The term minister, includes a clergyman, pastor, rector, priest, rabbi, or other person having authority from,
or in accordance with, the rules and regulations of the
governing ecclesiastical body of the denomination or
order, if any, to which the church belongs, or otherwise
from the church, to preside over and direct the spiritual
affairs of the church.—Chap. 723, Laws 1895.

INCORPORATION OF CHURCHES, GENERAL PROVISIONS.

Notice of meeting for incorporation.—Notice of a meeting for the purpose of incorporating an unincorporated church, to which this article is applicable, shall be given as follows:

The notice shall be in writing, and shall state, in substance, that a meeting of such unincorporated church will be held at its usual place of worship at a specified day and hour, for the purpose of incorporating such church and electing trustees thereof.

The notice must be signed by at least six persons of full age, who are then members in good and regular standing of such church by admission into full communion or membership therewith, in accordance with the rules and regulations of such church, and of the governing ecclesiastical body of the denomination or order, if any, to which the church belongs, or who have statedly worshiped with such church, and have regularly contributed to the financial support thereof during the year next prior thereto, or from the time of the formation thereof.

A copy of such notice shall be posted conspicuously on the outside of the main entrance to such place of worship, at least fifteen days before the day so specified for such meeting, and shall be publicly read at each of the two next preceding regular meetings of such unincorporated church for public worship, at least one week apart, at morning service, if such service be held, on Sunday, if Sunday be the day for such regular meetings, by the first-named of the following persons who is present thereat, to wit: The minister of such church, the officiating minister thereof, the elders thereof in the order of their age, beginning with the eldest, the deacons of the church in the order of the age, beginning with the eldest, any person qualified to sign such notice.—Chap. 723, Laws 1895.

The meeting for incorporation.—At the meeting for incorporation held in pursuance of such notice, the following persons, and no others, shall be qualified voters, to wit: All persons of full age, who are then members, in good and regular standing of such church by admission into full communion or membership therewith, in accordance with the rules and regulations thereof, and of the governing ecclesiastical body, if any, of the denomination, or order, to which the church belongs, or who have statedly worshiped with such church, and have regularly contributed to the financial support thereof during the year next preceding such meeting, or from the time of the formation thereof.

The presence of a majority of such qualified voters, at least six in number, shall be necessary to constitute a quorum of such meeting. The action of the meeting upon any matter or question shall be decided by a majority of the qualified voters voting thereon, a quorum being present.

The first-named of the following persons, who is present at such meeting, shall preside thereat, to wit: The minister of the church, the officiating minister thereof, the elders thereof in the order of their age, beginning with the eldest, the deacons thereof in the order of their age, beginning with the eldest, any qualified voter elected to preside. The presiding officer of the meeting shall receive the votes, be the judge of the qualifications of voters, and declare the result of the votes cast on any matter. The polls of his meeting shall remain open for one hour, and longer, in the discretion of the presiding officer, or, if required, by a majority of the voters present.

Such meeting shall decide whether such unincorporated church shall become incorporated. If such decision shall be in favor of incorporation, such meeting shall decide upon the name of the proposed corporation, the number of the trustees thereof, which shall be three, six, or nine, and shall determine the date, not more than fifteen months thereafter, on which the first annual election of the trustees thereof after such meeting shall be held. Such meeting shall elect from the persons qualified to vote at such meeting, one-third of the number of trustees so decided on, who shall hold office until the first annual election of trustees thereafter, one-third of such number of trustees to hold office until the second annual election of trustees thereafter, and one-third of such number of trustees to hold office until the third annual election of trustees thereafter.—Chap. 723, Laws 1895.

The certificate of incorporation. — The presiding officer of such meeting and at least two other persons present and voting thereat shall execute and acknowledge a certificate of incorporation, setting forth the matters so determined at such meeting, the trustees elected thereat, and the terms of office for which they were respectively elected, and the county, town, city, or village, in which its principal place of worship is or is intended to be located. On filing such certificate the members of such church and the persons qualified to vote at such meeting, and who shall thereafter from time to time be qualified voters at the corporate meetings thereof, shall be the corporation by the name stated in such certificate, and the persons therein stated to be elected trustees of such church shall be the trustees thereof, for the terms for which they were respectively so elected.—Chap. 723, Laws 1895.

Filing and recording certificates of incorporation of religious corporations. — The certificate of incorporation of a religious corporation shall be acknowledged or proved before an officer authorized to take the acknowledgment or proof of deeds or conveyances of real estate, to be recorded in the county in which the principal office or place of worship of said corporation is or is intended to be situated, and shall be filed and recorded in the office of the clerk of said county. If there is not, or is not intended to be, any such office or place of worship, the certificate shall be filed and recorded in the office of the Secretary of State.—Chap. 336, Laws 1896.

Time, place, and notice of corporate meetings. —The annual corporate meeting of every incorporated church to which these provisions are applicable shall be held at the time and place fixed by or in pursuance of law therefor, if such time and place be so fixed, and otherwise, at a time and place to be fixed by its trustees. A special corporate

meeting of any such church may be called by the board of
trustees thereof, on its own motion or on the written request of at least ten qualified voters of such church. The
trustees shall cause notice of the time and place of its
annual corporate meeting, therein specifying the names
of any trustees, whose successors are to be elected thereat,
and, if a special meeting, specifying the business to be
transacted thereat, to be given at a regular meeting of the
church for public worship, at morning service, if such service be held, on each of the two successive Sundays next
preceding such meeting, if Sunday be the regular day
for such public worship, and public worship be had thereon, or otherwise at a regular meeting of such church for
public worship on each of two days at least one week
apart next preceding such meeting, or if no such public
worship be held during such period, by conspicuously
posting such notice, in writing, upon the outer entrance
to the principal place of worship of such church. Such
notice shall be given by the minister of the church, if
there be one, or if not, or if any such minister refuse to
give such notice, by any officer of such church. But a
special corporate meeting of an incorporated Presbyterian church to elect a pastor of such church or to take action in reference to the dissolution of the relations of
the pastor and the church, may be only by the session
of such church. They may call such meeting whenever
they deem it advisable to do so, or upon the request to
them, by petition, of a majority of the qualified voters of
such corporation, they must call such meeting. They
shall give notice of such meeting in either case, in the
manner in which this chapter provided in a notice of a
special meeting.—Chap. 723, Laws 1895.

**Organization and conduct of corporate meetings; qualifi-
cation of voters thereat.**—At a corporate meeting of an
incorporated church to which these provisions are applicable, the following persons, and no others, shall be qualified voters, to wit: All persons of full age, who are then
members in good and regular standing of such church by
admission into full communion or membership there-

with, in accordance with the rules and regulations thereof, and of the governing ecclesiastical body, if any, of the denomination or order to which the church belongs, or who have been stated attendants on divine worship in such church, and have regularly contributed to the financial support thereof during the year next preceding such meeting; except that at a corporate meeting of any Methodist Episcopal church in the city of Brooklyn only persons who shall have been members thereof for at least one year prior thereto shall be qualified voters; and any incorporated church in connection with the Congregational denomination may at any annual corporate meeting thereof, if notice of the intention so to do has been given with the notice of such meeting, determine that thereafter only members of such church shall be qualified voters at corporate meetings thereof.

The presence at such meeting of at least six persons qualified to vote thereat shall be necessary to constitute a quorum. The action of the meeting upon any matter or question shall be decided by a majority of the qualified voters voting theron, a quorum being present.

The first named of the following persons who is present at such meeting shall preside thereat, to wit: The minister of such church, the officiating minister thereof, the officers thereof in the order of their age, beginning with the eldest, any qualified voters elected therefor at the meeting. The presiding officer of the meeting shall receive the votes, be the judge of the qualifications of voters, and declare the result of the votes cast on any matter. The polls of an annual corporate meeting shall continue open for one hour, and longer in the discretion of the presiding officer, or, if required, by a majority of the qualified voters present.

At each annual corporate meeting successors to those trustees whose terms of office then expire, shall be elected from the qualified voters by ballot, for a term of three years thereafter.—Chap. 723, Laws 1895.

Changing date of annual corporate meetings.—An annual corporate meeting of an incorporated church to

which these provisions are applicable may change the
date of its annual meeting thereafter. If such date shall
next thereafter occur less than six months after the annual meeting at which such change is made, the next annual meeting shall be held one year from such next re-
curring date. For the purpose of determining the terms
of office of trustees, the time between the annual meeting
at which such change is made, and the next annual meeting thereafter, shall be reckoned as one year.—Chap. 723,
Laws 1895.

Changing number of trustees.—An incorporated church
to which these provisions are applicable may, at an annual corporate meeting, change the number of its trustees
to three, six, or nine, or classify them so that the terms
of one-third expire each year. No such change shall affect the terms of the trustees then in office, and if the
change reduces the number of trustees, it shall not take
effect until the number of trustees whose terms of office
continue for one or more years after an annual election, is
less than the number determined upon. Whenever the
number of trustees so holding over is less than the number so determined on, trustees shall be elected in addition to those so holding over, sufficient to make the number of trustees for the ensuing year equal to the number
so determined on. The trustees so elected up to and
including one-third of the number so determined on,
shall be elected for three years, the remainder up to and
including one-third of the number so determined on for
two years, and the remainder for one year.—Chap. 723,
Laws 1895.

Meetings of trustees.—Two of the trustees of an incorporated church to which these provisions are applicable
may call a meeting of such trustees by giving at least
twenty-four hours' notice thereof personally or by mail to
the other trustees. A majority of the trustees lawfully
convened shall constitute a quorum for the transaction of
business. In case of a tie vote at a meeting of the trustees, the presiding officer of such meeting shall, notwith-

standing that he has voted once, have an additional casting vote.—Chap. 723, Laws 1895.

The creation and filling of vacancies among trustees of such churches.—If any trustee of an incorporated church to which these provisions are applicable declines to act, resigns, or dies, or, having been a member of such church, ceases to be such member, or not having been a member of such church, ceases to be a qualified voter at a corporate meeting thereof, his office shall be vacant, and such vacancy may be filled by the remaining trustees until the next annual corporate meeting of such church, at which meeting the vacancy shall be filled for the unexpired term.—Chap. 723, Laws 1895.

Control of trustees by corporate meetings of such churches.—A corporate meeting of an incorporated church whose trustees are elected as such, may give directions, not inconsistent with law, as to the manner in which any of the temporal affairs of the church shall be administered by the trustees thereof; and such directions shall be followed by the trustees. The trustees of an incorporated church to which these provisions are applicable shall have no power to settle, or remove, or fix the salary of the minister, or without the consent of a corporate meeting, to incur debts beyond what is necessary for the care of the property of the corporation; or to fix, or change the time, nature, or order of the public or social worship of such church, except when such trustees are also the spiritual officers of such church.—Chap. 723, Laws 1895.

Consolidation of incorporated Churches.—Two or more incorporated churches may enter into an agreement, under their respective corporate seals, for the consolidation of such corporations, setting forth the name of the proposed new corporation, the denomination, if any, to which it is to belong, and if the churches of such denomination have more than one method of choosing trustees, by which of such methods the trustees are to be chosen, the number of such trustees, the names of the persons to be the first trustees of the new corporation, and the date of its first annual corporate meeting. Such agreement shall not be valid unless approved by the governing body of the denomination, if any, to which each church belongs, having jurisdiction over such church. Each corporation shall thereupon make a separate petition to the supreme court for an order consolidating the corporation, setting forth the denomination, if any, to which the church belongs, that the consent of the governing body to the consolidation, if any, of that denomination having jurisdiction over such church has been obtained, the agreement therefor, and a statement of all the property and liabilities, and the amount and sources of the annual income of such petitioning organization. In its discretion the court may direct that notice of the hearing of such petition be given to the parties interested therein in such manner and for such time as it may prescribe. After hearing all the parties interested, present and desiring to be heard, the court may make an order for the consolidation of the corporations on the terms of such agreement, and such other terms and conditions as it may prescribe, specifying the name of such new corporation and the first trustees thereof, and the method by which their successors shall be chosen and the date of its first annual corporate meeting. When such order is made and duly entered, the persons constituting such corporations shall become an incorporated church by, and said petitioning churches shall become consolidated under, the name designated in the order, and the trustees therein named shall be the first trustees thereof, and the future trustees thereof shall be chosen by the method therein designated, and all the estate, rights, powers, and property of whatsoever nature, belonging to either corporation shall, without further act or deed, be vested and transferred to the new corporation as effectually as they were vested in or belonged to the former corporations; and the said new corporation shall be liable for all the debts and liabilities of the former corporations in the same manner and as effectually as if said debts or liabilities had been contracted or incurred by the new corporation. A certified copy of such order shall be recorded in the book for recording certificates of incorporation in each county clerk's office in which the certificate of incorporation of each consolidating church was recorded; or if no such certificate was so recorded, then in the clerk's office of the county in which the principal place of worship or principal office of the new corporation is, or is intended to be, situated.—Chap. 56, Laws 1896.

To maintain homes for their aged poor.—An incorporated church or congregation in this State, either by itself, or in conjunction with other incorporated churches or congregations, shall have power to establish and maintain by its or their trustees, or other officers, as part of its or their regular church and charitable work, a home for the aged poor of its or their membership or congregation, and may take and hold as joint tenants, tenants in common, or otherwise, by conveyance, donation, bequest, or device, real and personal property for such purpose, and may purchase and erect suitable buildings therefor.

Any such church or congregation, with other incorporated churches or congregations, may take and hold any grant, donation, bequest, or devise of real or personal property heretofore made, upon trust, and apply the same or the income thereof under the direction of the trustees or other officers having charge of the temporalities of such church, or churches, or congregation, or congregations, for the purpose of establishing or maintaining such a home, and for the erection, preservation, repair, or extension of any building or buildings for such purpose, upon such terms and conditions, and subject to such conditions, limitations, and restrictions, as shall be contained in the deed, will or other instrument or conveyance by which the property is given, transferred, or conveyed. This act shall take effect immediately.—Chap. 473, Laws 1898. Approved April 22.

Corporations for organizing and maintaining mission churches and Sunday-schools.—Ten or more members of two or more incorporated churches may become a corporation for the purpose of organizing and maintaining mis-

sion churches and Sunday-schools, and of acquiring property therefor, by executing a certificate stating the name
of such corporation, the city in which its principal office or
church or school is, or is intended to be, located; the number of trustees to manage its affairs, which shall be three,
six, or nine, and the names of the trustees for the first
year of its existence, which certificates shall be acknowledged or proved and filed as hereinbefore provided.
Whenever a mission church established by such corporation becomes self-sustaining, such mission-church may
become incorporated and shall be governed under the
provisions of this act for the incorporation and government of a church of the religious denomination to which
such mission church belongs, and thereon such parent
corporation may convey to such incorporated church the
property connected therewith.—Chap. 336, Laws 1896.

Corporations with governing authority over churches.—
An unincorporated diocesan convention, presbytery,
classis, synod, annual conference, or other ecclesiastical governing body, having jurisdiction over several
churches, may at a stated meeting thereof determine to
become incorporated by a designated name, and may by
a plurality vote elect not less than three nor more than
nine persons to be the first trustees of such corporation.
The presiding officer and clerk of such governing body
shall execute and acknowledge a certificate stating that
such proceedings were duly taken as herein provided, the
name by which such corporation is to be known, and the
names of such first trustees. On filing such certificate,
the members of such governing body and their successors shall be a corporation by the name stated in the certificate, and the persons named as trustees therein shall
be the first trustees thereof.

The trustees of every incorporated governing body and
their successors shall hold their offices during the pleasure of such body, which may remove them and fill vacancies in accordance with its rules and regulations. Such
corporation may take, administer, and dispose of property for the benefit of such governing body, or of any

parish, congregation, society, church, mission, religious, benevolent, charitable, or educational institution existing or acting under it.—Chap. 723, Laws 1895.

For the dissolution of religious societies, except in the City and County of New York.—Whenever any religious society incorporated by law shall cease to act in its corporate capacity and keep up the religious services, it shall be lawful for the supreme court of this State, upon the application of a majority of the trustees thereof incorporated by law, except in the city and county of New York, in case such court shall deem it proper so to do, to order and decree a dissolution of such religious society, and for that purpose to order and direct a sale and conveyance of any and all property belonging to such society, and after providing for the ascertaining and payment of the debts of such society, and the necessary costs and expenses of such sale and proceedings for dissolution, so far as the proceeds of such sale shall be sufficient to pay the same; such court may order and direct any surplus of such proceeds remaining after paying such debts, costs, and expenses, to be devoted and applied to any such religious, benevolent, or charitable objects or purposes as the said trustees may indicate by their petition and the said court may approve.

Such application to said court shall be made by petition, duly verified by said trustees, which petition shall state the particular reason or causes why such sale and dissolution are sought; the situation, condition, and estimated value of the property of said society or corporation, and the particular object or purposes to which it is proposed to devote any surplus of the proceeds of such property; and such petition shall, in all cases, be accompanied with proof that notice of the time and place of such intended application to said court has been duly published once in each week for at least four weeks successively, next preceding such application, in a newspaper published in the county where such society is located.

In case there shall be no trustees of such religious society residing in the county in which such society is located, such application may be made, and such proceedings taken, by a majority of the members of such religious society residing in such county.

Application of this chapter to churches incorporated prior to January first, eighteen hundred and twenty-eight. —Any provision of this chapter (723, Laws 1895) shall not be deemed to apply to any church incorporated under any general or special law, prior to January first, eighteen hundred and twenty-eight, if such provision is inconsistent with or in derogation of any of the rights and privileges of such corporation, as they existed under the law by or pursuant to which such corporation was formed, unless such corporation subsequent to such date, shall have lawfully reincorporated under a law enacted since the first day of January, eighteen hundred and twenty-eight, or unless the trustees of such corporation shall, by resolution, determine that the provisions of this chapter applying to churches of the same denomination and to the trustees thereof shall apply to such church, and unless such resolution shall be submitted to the next ensuing annual meeting of such church, and be ratified by a majority of the votes of the qualified voters present and voting thereon. Notice of the adoption of such resolution and of the proposed submission thereof for ratification, shall be given with the notice of such annual meeting, and, in addition thereto, mailed to each member of such church corporation at his last known postoffice address, at least two weeks prior to such annual meeting, and published once a week for two successive weeks immediately preceding such meeting in a newspaper, if any, published in the city, village, or town in which the principal place of worship of such corporation is located, and otherwise in a newspaper published in an adjoining town. If such resolution is so ratified, the trustees of such church shall cause a certificate setting forth a copy of such resolution, its adoption by the board of trustees, and its due ratification by the members of such corporation, to be filed in the office of the clerk of the county in which the principal place of worship of such

corporation is located. Such county clerk shall cause
such certificate to be recorded in the book in which certificates of incorporation of religious corporations are
recorded in pursuance of law.—Chap. 336, Laws 1896.

**Application of this chapter to churches created by
special laws.**—If a church be incorporated by special law,
it and its trustees shall have, in addition to the powers
conferred on it by such law, all the powers and privileges
conferred on incorporated churches, and the trustees
thereof respectively by the provisions of this article, and
also all the powers and privileges conferred by this chapter on churches of the same denomination, or of the like
character, and on the trustees thereof respectively.—
Chap. 723, Laws 1895.

Where the original certificate of incorporation of a religious society is lost, a copy of the record thereof, duly
certified by the clerk of the county, will properly be admitted in evidence. It is sufficient that the official character of the officer taking the acknowledgment appears
in the body of the certificate. An acknowledgment before a commissioner of deeds has the same force and val-
idity as if taken before one of the officers named in the
first section of the act of eighteen hundred and thirteen
providing for the incorporation of religious societies.
Second Methodist Episcopal Church of Greenwich *vs.*
Humphrey, 49 St. Rep., 467.

General powers and duties of trustees of religious corporations.

— The trustees of every religious corporation shall have the custody and control of all the temporalities and property, real or personal, belonging to the corporation, and of the revenues therefrom, and shall administer the same in accordance with the discipline, rules, and usages of the corporation and of the ecclesiastical governing body, if any, to which the corporation is subject, and with the provisions of the law relating thereto, for the support and maintenance of the corporation; or, providing the members of the corporation at a meeting thereof shall so authorize, of some religious, charitable, benevolent, or educational object conducted by said corporation or in connection with it, or with the denomination, if any, with which it is connected; and they shall not use such property or revenues for any other purpose or divert the same from such uses. By-laws may be adopted and amended, by a two-thirds vote of the qualified voters present and voting at the meeting for incorporation, or at any subsequent meeting, after written notice, embodying such by-laws or amendment, has been openly given at a previous meeting, and also in the notices of the meeting at which such proposed by-law or amendment is to be acted upon. By-laws thus adopted or amended shall control the action of the trustees. But this section does not give the trustees of an incorporated church any control over the calling, settlement, dismissal, or removal of its minister, or the fixing of his salary; or any power to fix or change the times, nature, or order of the public or social worship of such church.—Chap. 621, Laws 1897.

Where the question is as to the legal rights of rival claimants to a trusteeship of a religious corporation, the claimants who have been in recognized possession may be sustained by a writ of injunction to restrain any disorderly interference by the other claimants until the legal right may be settled by an action, brought by the Attorney-

General in the name of the people. Reis *vs.* Rohde, 34
Hun., 161.

When a right of property is dependent upon a question
of doctrine, discipline, or church government, a civil court
where the question may arise will treat the determination
made upon such question by the highest tribunal within
the church organization as controlling in that respect.
Beyond that there can be no recognition in this State of
the jurisdiction and judicial power of any ecclesiastical
court. Questions of the civil rights of persons relating to
themselves personally or to property, whatever may be
their relations to church organizations, are subjects for
adjudication by the civil tribunals exclusively. The civil
courts do not interfere with ecclesiastical matters in
which temporal rights are not involved. Baxter v. Mc-
Donnell, 18 App. Div., 235, 1897.

To perfect the relation of pastor—that is, of permanent
pastor, there must be an unqualified offer to the proposed
incumbent, and an unqualified acceptance of the offer.

The trustees of a religious corporation may be enjoined,
in an action brought by a trustee, from paying the pastor
the salary of a permanent pastor, or otherwise treating
him as such when he is only acting pastor; from interfering with the rights of church members to meet in the
church building by themselves, and from interfering with
the power of self-government of the church or of the society; from attempting to prescribe new qualifications of
voters at the meetings of the church or society, and from
excluding any of their number from access to their books
and records.

An acting pastor, who is neither a member of the church
nor of the society, may be enjoined from assuming to interfere as an officer thereof, contrary to its customary
usages. Hopkins *vs.* Seymour, N. Y. Super. Ct., Sp. T.,
1884.

A pewholder, as between himself and the legal owners
of the church edifice, has only the right to occupy his pew
during divine service. This right is subordinate to the
right of the corporation to remodel the building, or to sell

it and remove elsewhere. Erwin *vs.* Hurd, 133 Abb. N. C., 91.

Upon the sale of a church and the erection of a new one, it is the duty of the trustees to tender a pewholder a pew in the new edifice corresponding in location to that which he owned in the former building, upon the payment of such a sum as, in equity, he ought to pay, if the cost of the new structure exceeds the proceeds of the sale of the old property, together with the sums in the treasury of the society, and if they fail so to do, he should be indemnified for his loss. Sup. Ct., 1893. Mayer *vs.* Temple Beth. El. 23 N. Y. Supp., 1013.

A religious corporation is not liable for injuries sustained by reason of the negligence of an employee, in the absence of proof that the employee was not qualified for the work he was engaged to perform, or that there was negligence of the corporation's officers in his selection. Haas *vs.* Missionary Society of the Most Holy Redeemer. 26 N. Y. Supp., 868.

CHURCH PROPERTY.

Limitations upon property and Income of religious corporations; inheritance tax not applicable.—Any religious, educational, Bible, missionary, tract, literary, scientific, benevolent, or charitable corporation, or corporation organized for the enforcement of laws relating to children or animals, or for hospital, infirmary, or other new business purposes, may take and hold, in its own right, or in trust for any other purpose comprised in the objects of its incorporation, property not exceeding in value three million dollars, or the yearly income derived from which shall not exceed two hundred and fifty thousand dollars, notwithstanding the provisions of any special or general act heretofore passed or certificate of incorporation affecting such corporations. In computing the value of such property no increase in value arising otherwise than from improvements made thereon, shall be taken into account. The personal estate of such corporations shall be exempt from taxation, and the provisions of chapter four hundred and eighty-three of the laws of eighteen hundred and eighty-five, entitled, "An act to tax gifts, legacies, and collateral inheritances in certain cases," and the acts amendatory thereof, shall not apply thereto, nor to any gifts to any such corporation by grant, bequest, or otherwise; provided, however, that this provision shall not apply to any moneyed or stock corporations deriving an income or profit from the capital or otherwise, or to any corporation which has the right to make dividends or to distribute profits or assets among its members.

This act shall not affect the right of any such corporation to take and hold property exceeding in value the amount specified in this act, provided such right is conferred upon such corporation by special statute; nor affect any statute by which its real estate is exempt from taxation.—Chap. 553, Laws 1890.

Property of unincorporated society transferred by its incorporation. — All the temporalities and property of an unincorporated church, or of any unincorporated religious

society, body, association, or congregation, shall on the
incorporation thereof, become the temporalities and property of such corporation whether such temporalities or
property be given, granted, or devised directly to such unincorporated church, society, body, association, or congregation, or to any other person for the use or benefit
thereof.—Chap. 723, Laws 1895.

**Correction and confirmation of conveyances to relig-
ious corporations.**—If, in a conveyance of real property,
or in any instrument intended to operate as such, heretofore or hereafter made to a religious corporation, its corporate name is not stated or is not correctly stated, but
such conveyance or instrument indicates the intention
of the grantor therein to convey such property to such
corporation, and such corporation has entered into possession and occupation of such property, any officer of the
corporation authorized so to do by its trustees may record
in the office where such conveyance or instrument is recorded a statement, signed and acknowledged by him or
proved, setting forth the date of such conveyance or instrument, the date of record, and the number and page of
the book of record thereof, the name of the grantor, a
description of the property conveyed or intended to be
conveyed, the name of the grantee as expressed in such
conveyance or instrument, the correct name of such corporation, the fact of authorization, by the trustees of the
corporation, to make and record such statement, and that
the grantor in such conveyance or instrument intended
thereby to convey such property to such corporation as
the said officer verily believes, with the reason for such
belief. Such statement so signed and acknowledged or
proved shall be recorded with the records of deeds in such
office, and indexed as a deed from the grantee as named
in such instrument or in such conveyance to such corporation. The register, or clerk, as the case may be shall
note the recording of such statement on the margin of the
record of such conveyance, and for his services shall be
entitled to receive the fees allowed for recording deeds.
Such statements so recorded shall be presumptive evi-

dence that such matters therein stated are true, and that
such corporation was the grantee in the original instrument or conveyance. All conveyances heretofore made, or
by any instrument intended to be made, to a religious corporation of real property appropriated to the use of such
corporation, or entitled to be so appropriated, are hereby
confirmed and declared valid and effectual, notwithstanding any defect in the form of the conveyance or the description of the grantee therein, but this section shall
not affect any suit or proceeding pending on the thirty-
first day of January, eighteen hundred and seventy-one.
—Chap. 336, Laws 1896.

**Judicial investigation of amount of property of re-
ligious corporations.**—The supreme court at a special
term, held in the judicial district in which the principal
place of worship or of holding corporate meetings of a
religious corporation is situated, may require such corporation to make and file an inventory of its property,
verified by its trustees, or a majority of them, on the
written application of the attorney-general, stating that,
from his knowledge, or on information and belief, the
value of the property held by such corporation exceeds
the amount authorized by law. On presentation of such
application, the court shall order that a notice of at least
eight days, together with a copy of the application, be
served upon the trustees of the corporation, requiring
them to show cause at a time and place therein specified
why they should not make and file such inventory and
account. If, on the hearing of such application, no good
cause is shown to the contrary, the court may make an
order requiring such inventory or account to be filed,
and may also proceed to take and state the amount of
property held by the corporation, and may appoint a
referee for that purpose; and when such account is taken
and stated, after hearing all the parties appearing on the
application, the court may enter an order determining
the amount of property so held by the corporation and its
annual income, from which order an appeal may be taken
by any party aggrieved as from a judgment of the su-

preme court in an action tried therein before a court
without a jury.   No corporation shall be required to
make and file more than one inventory and account in any
one year, or to make a second account and inventory
while proceedings are pending for the statement of an
account under this section.—Chap. 723. Laws 1895.

**Acquisition of property by religious corporations for
branch institutions; establishment, maintenance, and management thereof.**— Any religious corporation may acquire property for associate houses, church buildings,
chapels, mission-houses, schoolhouses for Sunday or
parochial schools, or dispensaries of medicine for the poor,
or property for the residence of its ministers, teachers, or
employees, or property for a home for the aged.   The persons attending public worship in any such associate
house, mission-house, church building, or chapel connected therewith shall not, by reason thereof, have any
rights as members of the parent corporation.   The persons statedly worshiping in such house, mission-house,
church building, or chapel, may, with the consent of the
trustees of such corporation, become separately incorporated as a church, and the parent corporation may, in
pursuance of the provisions of law regulating the disposition of real property by religious corporations, rent or
convey to the new corporation, with or without consideration, any such associate house, church building, chapel,
mission-house, schoolhouse, or dispensary, and the lot
connected therewith, subject to such regulations as the
trustees of the parent corporation may make.   Any religious corporation shall have power to establish, maintain, and manage, by its trustees, or other officers as a
part of its religious purpose, a home for the aged, and may
take and hold by conveyance, donation, bequest, or devise,
real and personal property for such purpose, and may
purchase and may erect suitable buildings therefor.   Any
such corporation may take and hold in grant, donation,
bequest, or devise of real or personal property heretofore or hereafter made upon trust, apply the same, or the
income thereof, under the direction of its trustees or other

officers, for the purpose of establishing, maintaining, and managing such a home, and for the erection, preservation, repair, or extension of any building or buildings for such purpose.—Chap. 525, Laws 1896.

Acquisition of property by two or more religious corporations for a common parsonage.—Two or more religious corporations may acquire such real property as may be necessary for use as a parsonage, and the right, title, and interest of each corporation therein shall be in proportion to its contribution to the cost of such property. The trustees of each corporation shall, from time to time, appoint one of their number to be a trustee of such common parsonage property, to hold office during the pleasure of the appointing trustees, or until his successor be appointed. The trustees so appointed shall have the care and management of such property and may make such improvements thereupon as they deem necessary, and determine the proportion of the expense of the maintenance thereof which each corporation shall bear. If at any time either of such corporations acquires or desires to acquire for its own exclusive use as a parsonage other real property, it may, in pursuance of the provisions of law relating to the disposition of real property by religious corporations, sell and convey its interest in such common parsonage property to any one or more of the other corporations having an interest therein.—Chap. 723, Laws 1895.

Acquisition of property by religious corporations for cemetery purposes ; management thereof.—A religious corporation may take and hold, by purchase, grant, gift, or devise, real property for the purposes of a cemetery; or such lot or lots in any cemetery connected with it, as may be conveyed or devised to it, with or without provisions limiting interments therein to particular persons or classes of persons; and may take and hold any property granted, given, devised, or bequeathed to it in trust to apply the same, or the income or proceeds thereof, under the direction of the trustees of the corporation, for the improvement or embellishment of such cemetery or any lot therein, including the erection. repair, preservation, or removal of tombs. monuments, gravestones, fences, railings, or other erections, or the planting or cultivation of trees, shrubs, plants, or flowers in and around any such cemetery or cemetery lots.

A religious corporation may erect upon any property held by it for cemetery purposes, a suitable building for religious services for the burial of the dead, or for the use of the keepers or other persons employed in connection therewith, and may sell or convey lots in such cemetery for burial purposes, subject to such conditions and restrictions as may be imposed by the instrument by which the same was acquired, or by the rules and regulations adopted by such corporation.   Every such conveyance of a lot or plat for burial purposes. signed, sealed, and acknowledged in the same manner as a deed to be recorded, may be recorded in like manner and with like effect as a deed of real property.—Chap. 723, Laws 1895.

Sale, mortgage, and lease of real property of religious corporations. — A religious corporation shall not sell or mortgage any of its real property without applying to and obtaining leave of the court therefor.

The trustees of an incorporated Protestant Episcopal church shall not vote upon any resolution or proposition for the sale. mortgage, or lease of its real property, unless the rector of such church, if it then has a rector, shall be present.

The trustees of an incorporated Roman Catholic church shall not make application to the court for leave to mortgage, lease, or sell any of its real property without the consent of the Archbishop or Bishop of the diocese to which such church belongs, or in case of their absence or inability to act, without the consent of the Vicar-General or administrator of such diocese.

The petition of the trustees of an incorporated Protestant Episcopal church, or a Roman Catholic church shall, in addition to the matters required by the Civil Code to be set forth therein, set forth that this section has also been complied with.

But lots, plats, or burial permits in a cemetery owned by a religious corporation may be sold without applying for or obtaining leave of the court.

No cemetery lands of a religious corporation shall be mortgaged while used for cemetery purposes.—Chap. 723, Laws 1895.

Property of extinct churches.—An incorporated governing body may decide that a church, parish, or society in connection with it, or over which it has ecclesiastical jurisdiction, has become extinct, if it has failed for two consecutive years prior thereto, to maintain religious services according to the discipline, customs, and usages of such governing body, or has had less than thirteen resident attending members paying annual pew rent, or making annual contribution toward its support, and may take possession of the temporalities and property belonging to such church, parish, or religious society, and manage; or may, in pursuance of the provisions of law relating to the disposition of real property by religious corporations, sell or dispose of the same and apply the proceeds thereof to any of the purposes to which the property of such governing body is devoted, and it shall not divert such property to any other object. The New York Eastern Christian Benevolent and Missionary Society shall be deemed the governing religious body of any extinct or disbanded church of the Christian denomination situated within the bounds of the New York Eastern Christian conference; and the New York Christian Association, of any other church of the Christian denomination, and any other incorporated conference shall be deemed the governing religious body of any church situated within its bounds. By Christian denomination is meant only the denomination especially termed " Christian," in which the Bible is declared to be the only rule of faith, Christian their only name, and Christian character their only test of fellowship, and in which no form of baptism is made a test of Christian character.—Chap. 238, Laws 1897.

Mortmain restrictions.—No person having a husband, wife, child, or parent, shall, by his or her last will and a test of Christian character.

testament, devise or bequeath to any benevolent, charitable, literary, scientific, or religious, or missionary society, association, or corporation in trust or otherwise, more than one-half part of his or her estate, after the payment of his or her debts (and such devise or bequest shall be valid to the extent of one-half and no more).—Chap. 360, Laws 1860.

Places in which traffic in liquor shall not be permitted. —* * * in any building, yard, booth, or other place which shall be on the same street or avenue and within two hundred feet of a building occupied exclusively as a church or school-house; the measurements to be taken from the center of the nearest entrance of the building used for such church or school-house to the center of the nearest entrance of the place in which such liquor traffic is desired to be carried on; provided, however, that this prohibition shall not apply to a place which is occupied for a hotel, nor to a place in which such traffic in liquors is actually lawfully carried on when this act takes effect, nor to a place which at such date is occupied, or in process of construction, by a corporation or association which traffics in liquors solely with the members thereof, nor to a place within such limit to which a corporation or association trafficing in liquors solely with the members thereof when this act takes effect may remove; provided, however, such place to which such corporation or association may so remove, shall be located within two hundred feet of the place in which such corporation or association so traffics in liquors when this act takes effect.—Chap. 112, Laws 1896.

Exemption from taxation. — The following property shall be exempt from taxation:

All property exempt by law from execution, other than an exempt homestead.

The real property of a corporation or association organized exclusively for the moral or mental improvement of men or women, or for religious, Bible, tract, charitable, benevolent, missionary, hospital, infirmary, educational, scientific, literary, library, patriotic, historical, or cemetery purposes, or for the enforcement of laws relating to children or animals, or for two or more of such purposes, and used exclusively for carrying out thereupon one or more of such purposes, and the personal property of any such corporation or association shall be exempt from taxation.

But no such corporation or association shall be entitled to any such exemption if any officer, member, or employee thereof shall receive or may be lawfully entitled to receive any pecuniary profit from the operations thereof, excepting reasonable compensation for services in effecting one or more of such purposes, or as property beneficiaries of its strictly charitable purposes; or if the organization thereof, for any of such avowed purposes, be a guise or pretense for directly or indirectly making any other pecuniary profit for such corporation or association, or for any of its members or employees, or if it be not in good faith organized or conducted exclusively for one or more of such purposes. The real property of any such corporation or association entitled to such exemption held by it exclusively for one or more of such purposes, and from which no rents, profits or incomes are derived, shall be so exempt, though not in actual use therefor, by reason of the absence of suitable buildings or improvements thereon, if the construction of such buildings or improvements is in progress, or is in good faith contemplated by such corporation or association. The real property of any such corporation not so used exclusively for carrying out thereupon one or more of such purposes, but leased or otherwise used for other purposes, shall not be so exempt; but if a portion only of any lot or building of any such corporation or association is used exclusively for carrying out thereupon one or more of such purposes of any such corporation or association, then such lot or building shall be so exempt only to the extent of the value of the portion so used, and the remaining portion of such lot or building to the extent of the value of such remaining portion shall be subject to taxation. Property held by an officer of a religious denomination shall be entitled to the same exemptions, subject to the same conditions and exceptions as property held by a religious corporation.

All dwelling houses and lots of religious corporations while actually used by the officiating clergymen thereof, but the total amount of such exemption to any one religious corporation shall not exceed two thousand dollars. Such exemption shall be in addition to that provided by subdivision seven of this section.

The real property of a minister of the gospel or priest who is regularly engaged in performing his duties as such, or permanently disabled, by impaired health from the performance of such duties, or over seventy-five years of age, and the personal property of such minister or priest, but the total amount of such exemption on account of both real and personal property shall not exceed fifteen hundred dollars.—Chap. 908, Laws 1896.

Lands set apart for the erection of a church are not exempt from taxation until the building is actually commenced. "The law," says Judge Roosevelt in Trinity Church *vs.* Mayor, 10 How. Pr., 138, " to warrant this claim of privilege, requires an actual building—a house made with hands—not eternal in the heavens, but temporal, situated on temporal lots, resting not on intention, however pious and praiseworthy, but on solid, sublunary earth."

Notice of meeting for incorporation.—Notice of a meeting for the purpose of incorporating an unincorporated Baptist church shall be given as follows: The notice shall be in writing, and shall state, in substance, that a meeting of such unincorporated church will be held at its usual place of worship at a specified day and hour, for the purpose of incorporating such church, electing trustees thereof, and selecting a corporate name therefor. The notice must be signed by at least six persons of full age, who are then members in good and regular standing of such church by admission into full communion or membership therewith. A copy of such notice shall be publicly read at a regular meeting of such unincorporated church for public worship, on the two successive Sundays immediately preceding the meeting, by the minister of such church, or a deacon thereof or by any person qualified to sign such notice.

The meeting for incorporation.—At the meeting for incorporation, held in pursuance of such notice, the qualified voters, until otherwise decided as hereinafter provided, shall be all persons of full age, who are then members, in good and regular standing of such church, by admission into full communion or membership therewith. At such meeting the presence of a majority of such qualified voters, at least six in number, shall be necessary to constitute a quorum, and all matters or questions shall be decided by a majority of the qualified voters voting thereon. There shall be elected at said meeting from the qualified voters then present, a presiding officer, a clerk to keep the record of the proceedings of the meeting and two inspectors of election to receive the ballots cast. The presiding officer and the inspectors shall declare the result of the ballots cast on any matter, and shall be the judges of the qualifications of voters. If the meeting shall decide that such unincorporated church shall become incorporated, the meeting shall also decide upon the name of the proposed corporation, the number of the trustees thereof.

which shall be three, six, or nine, and the date, not more than fifteen months thereafter, on which the first annual election of the trustees thereof shall be held, and shall decide also whether those who, from the time of the formation of such church or during the year preceding the meeting for incorporation, have statedly worshiped with such church and have regularly contributed to the financial support thereof, shall be qualified voters at such meeting for incorporation, and whether those who, during the year preceding the subsequent corporate meetings of the church shall have statedly worshiped with such church and shall have regularly contributed to the financial support thereof, shall be qualified voters at such corporate meetings. Such meeting shall thereupon elect by ballot from the persons qualified to vote thereat one-third of the number of trustees so decided on, who shall hold office until the first annual election of trustees thereafter, and one-third of such number of trustees who shall hold office until the second annual election of trustees thereafter, and one-third of such number of trustees who shall hold office until the third annual election of trustees thereafter, or until the respective successors of such trustees shall be elected.

The certificate of incorporation.—If the meeting shall decide that such unincorporated church shall become incorporated, the presiding officer of such meeting and the two inspectors of elections shall execute a certificate setting forth the name of the proposed corporation, the number of the trustees thereof, the names of the persons elected as trustees, and the terms of office for which they were respectively elected, and the county and town, city, or village in which its principal place of worship is or is intended to be located. On the filing and recording of such certificate after it shall have been acknowledged or proved as hereinbefore provided, the persons qualified to vote at such meeting and those persons who shall thereafter, from time to time, be qualified voters at the corporate meetings thereof, shall be a corporation by the name stated in such certificate, and the persons therein stated to be elected trustees of such church shall be the trustees thereof, for the terms for which they were respectively elected and until their respective successors shall be elected.

Time, place, and notice of corporate meetings.—The annual corporate meeting of every incorporated Baptist church shall be held at the time and place fixed by or in pursuance of law therefor, if such time and place be so fixed, and otherwise, at a time and place to be fixed by its trustees. A special corporate meeting of any such church may be called by the board of trustees thereof, on its own motion, and shall be called on the written request of at least ten qualified voters of such church. The trustees shall cause notice of the time and place of its annual corporate meeting, and of the names of any trustees whose successors are to be elected thereat; and, if a special meeting, of the business to be transacted thereat, to be publicly read by the minister of such church or any trustee thereof at a regular meeting of the church for public worship, on the two successive Sundays immediately preceding such meeting.

Organization and conduct of corporate meetings; qualifications of voters thereat.—At a corporate meeting of an incorporated Baptist church the qualified voters shall be all persons of full age, who are then members of such church in good and regular standing by admission into full communion or membership therewith, or who have statedly worshiped with such church and have regularly contributed to the financial support thereof during the year next preceding such meeting; but any incorporated Baptist church may at any annual corporate meeting thereof, if notice of the intention so to do has been given with the notice of such meeting, decide that thereafter only members of such church of full age and in good and regular standing by admission into full communion or membership therewith shall be qualified voters at the corporate meetings. At such corporate meetings the presence of at least six persons qualified to vote thereat shall be necessary to constitute a quorum, and all matters or questions shall be decided by a majority of the qualified voters voting thereon. There shall be elected at said meeting from the qualified voters then present, a presiding officer, a clerk to keep the records of the proceedings of the meeting, and two inspectors of election to receive the ballots cast. The presiding officer and the inspectors of election shall declare the result of the ballots cast on any matter and shall be the judges of the qualifications of voters. At each annual corporate meeting, successors to those trustees whose terms of office then expire, shall be elected by ballot from the qualified voters, for a term of three years thereafter, and until their successors shall be elected.

Changing date of annual corporate meetings.—An annual corporate meeting of an incorporated Baptist church may change the date of its annual meeting thereafter. If the date fixed for the annual meeting shall be less than six months after the annual meeting at which such change is made, the next annual meeting shall be held one year from the date so fixed. For the purpose of determining the terms of office of trustees, the time between the annual meeting at which such change is made and the next annual meeting thereafter shall be reckoned as one year.

Changing number of trustees.—An incorporated Baptist church may, at an annual corporate meeting, change the number of its trustees to three, six, or nine, or classify them so that the terms of one-third expire each year, provided that notice of such intended change or classification be included in the notice of such annual corporate meeting. No such change shall affect the terms of the trustees then in office, and if the change reduces the number of trustees, elections shall not be held to fill vacancies caused by the expiration of the terms of trustees until the number of trustees equals the number to which the trustees were reduced. Whenever the number of trustees in office is less than the number so determined on, sufficient additional trustees shall be elected to make the number of trustees equal to the number so determined on. The trustees so elected up to and including one-third of the number so determined on, shall be elected for three years, the remainder up to and including one-third of the number so determined on for two years, and the remainder for one year.

Meetings of trustees.—Meetings of the trustees of an incorporated Baptist church shall be called by giving at least twenty-four hours' notice thereof personally or by mail to all the trustees, and such notice may be given by two of the trustees, but by the unanimous consent of the trustees a meeting may be held without previous notice thereof. A majority of the whole number of trustees shall constitute a quorum for the transaction of business at any meeting lawfully convened.

The creation and filling of vacancies among trustees of such churches.—If any trustee of an incorporated Baptist church declines to act, resigns, or dies, or having been a member of such church ceases to be such member, or not having been a member of such church, ceases to be a qualified voter at a corporate meeting thereof, his office shall be vacant, and such vacancy may be filled by the remaining trustees until the next annual corporate meeting of such church, at which meeting the vacancy shall be filled for the unexpired term.

Property of extinct Baptist Churches.—All the property, both real and personal, belonging to or held in trust for any Baptist church or Baptist religious society organized under the laws of the State of New York, that has become or shall become extinct, shall vest in and become the property of the Baptist Missionary Convention of the State of New York, and its successors or assigns; provided, that this act shall not affect the reversionary interests of any person or persons in such property, nor the interests of any incorporated association; and any Baptist church or Baptist religious society becoming extinct or about to disband or disorganize may, by a vote of two-thirds of its members present and voting therefor at a meeting regularly called for that purpose, assign, transfer, grant and convey all its temporalities to and place the same in the possession of the Baptist Missionary Convention of the State of New York.

Any Baptist church or Baptist religious society which has failed for two consecutive years next prior thereto to maintain religious services according to the custom and usages of Baptist churches, or has less than thirteen resident attending members, paying annual pew rental or making annual contributions toward its support, may be declared extinct in the following manner, viz.: Upon such notice as the court may prescribe, and upon application made by petition, stating fully the facts in the case, and on evidence being furnished that the said Baptist church or Baptist religious society has ceased to hold services in and use said property for religious worship or services for a term of two years previous to such application, the supreme court, at a term thereof held in the judicial district where such property is situated, may grant an order, declaring such church or society extinct, and thereon direct that all its temporalities shall be transferred to, and thereupon shall be taken possession of by the Baptist Missionary Convention of the State of New York, or directing that the same be sold in the manner directed by said order, and that the proceeds thereof, after payment of the debts of such church or society, be paid over to the Baptist Missionary Convention of the State of New York. All property and proceeds from the sale of property so transferred to said convention shall be used and applied for the purposes for which said Baptist Missionary Convention of the State of New York was organized, and shall not be directed to any other purpose.— Chap. 642, Laws 1894.

Baptist Missionary Convention.—All such persons as now are or hereafter may become members of the "Baptist Missionary Convention of the State of New York" shall be and hereby are constituted a body corporate by the name of the "Baptist Missionary Convention of the State of New York" for the purpose of propagating and spreading the Gospel, for the purpose of establishing, assisting, or maintaining in the State of New York, Baptist churches or missions or Sunday-schools for the study of the Scriptures, for the acquisition of sites in contemplation of the erection of houses of worship and other buildings, and to encourage and assist the educational interests of the Baptist denomination within the State.

It shall be lawful for the members of said corporation at any time they may elect to appoint such officers and such managers or directors, and to make and ordain such by-laws and regulations in regard to their organization and to the management, disposition, and sale of their real or personal estate, the duties and powers of their officers, managers, or directors, and the management of their corporate affairs, as they from time to time shall think proper, provided they are not inconsistent with the constitution and laws of this State and of the United States.

The said corporation shall have power to receive, take, hold, and enjoy any property, real or personal, by virtue of any devise, bequest, gift, grant, or purchase, either absolutely or in trust, and to make investments thereof, or of any of its funds, whenever and in such manner as it may deem advisable, and therewith to acquire or erect for its own use or accommodation, or for other purposes, such building or buildings as it may regard advantageous to the interests of the corporation or of the Baptist denomination with which it is connected, and to make sales, conveyances or mortgages of any of its real estate whenever and in such manner as it may deem advisable; subject only, however, in respect to the amount of property it may take and hold to the restrictions and limitations of existing laws, and in respect to devises or bequests from residents of the State of New York, to the provisions of Chap. 360, Laws of 1860, entitled " An Act in relation to Wills."

All the property, real and personal, heretofore in any manner acquired by the said " Baptist Missionary Convention of the State of New York," shall be deemed vested in the said corporation.

This act is hereby declared to be a public act, and the same shall be construed in all courts and places favorably for every purpose therein expressed or intended.

This act shall take effect immediately. Chap. 143, Laws 1898.

Free Baptist Churches.—All the property, both real and personal, belonging to or held in trust for any Free Baptist Church, or Free Baptist religious society organized under the laws of the State of New York, that has become or shall become extinct, shall vest in and become the property of the Central Association existing under the laws of the State of New York, and its successors and assigns; provided that this act shall not affect the reversionary interests of any person or persons in such property, nor the interests of any incorporated association; and any Free Baptist Church or Free Baptist religious society becoming extinct or about to disband or disorganize may, by a vote of two-thirds of its members present and voting therefor at a meeting regularly called for that purpose, assign, transfer, grant, and convey all its temporalities to, and place the same in the possession of the Central Association existing under the laws of the State of New York.

Any Free Baptist Church or Free Baptist religious society which has failed for two consecutive years next prior thereto to maintain religious services according to the custom and usages of Free Baptist churches, or has less than thirteen resident attending members, paying annual pew rental or making annual contributions toward its support, may be declared extinct in the following manner, viz.: Upon such notice as the court may prescribe, and upon application by petition, stating fully the facts in the case, and on evidence being furnished that the said Free Baptist Church or Free Baptist religious society has ceased to hold religious services in and use said property for religious worship or service for a term of two years previous to such application, the Supreme Court, at a term thereof held in the judicial district where such property is situated, may grant an order declaring such church or society extinct, and thereon direct that all its temporalities shall be transferred to and thereupon shall be taken possession of by the Central Association of the

State of New York, or directing that the same be sold in
the manner directed by said order, and that the proceeds
thereof, after the payment of the debts of such church or
society, be paid over to the Central Association of the
State of New York. All property and proceeds from the
sale of property so transferred to said association shall
be used and applied for the purposes for which said Central Association of the State of New York was organized,
and shall not be diverted to any other purpose.

The First Free Will Baptist Church of the City of New
York, located in the borough of Manhattan, shall in no
way be amenable to the provisions of this act.

This act shall take effect immediately. Chap. 248,
Laws 1898.

CONGREGATIONAL CHURCHES.

Notice of meeting for incorporation.—Notice of a meeting for the purpose of incorporating an unincorporated Congregational or Independent church shall be given as follows: The notice shall be in writing, and shall state, in substance, that a meeting of such unincorporated church will be held at its usual place of worship at a specified day and hour, for the purpose of incorporating such church, electing trustees therefor, and selecting a corporate name therefor. The notice must be signed by at least six persons of full age, who have statedly worshiped with such church, and have regularly contributed to its support, according to its usages, for at least one year, or since it was formed. A copy of such notice shall be publicly read at a regular meeting of such unincorporated church for public worship, on the two successive Sundays immediately preceding the meeting, by the minister of such church, or a deacon thereof, or by any person qualified to sign such notice.

The meeting for incorporation.—At the meeting for incorporation, held in pursuance of such notice, the qualified voters, until otherwise decided as hereinafter provided, shall be all persons of full age who have statedly worshiped with such church and have regularly contributed to its support, according to its usages, for at least one year, or since it was formed. At such meeting the presence of a majority of such qualified voters, at least six in number, shall be necessary to constitute a quorum, and all matters or questions shall be decided by a majority of the qualified voters voting thereon. The meeting shall be called to order by one of the signers of the call. There shall be elected at such meeting, from the qualified voters then present, a presiding officer, a clerk to keep the record of proceedings of the meeting, and two inspectors of election to receive the ballots cast. The presiding officer and the inspectors shall decide the result of the ballots cast. The presiding officer and the inspectors shall decide the result of the ballots cast on any matter, and shall be the judges of the qualifications of the voters. If the meeting shall decide that such unincorporated church shall become incorporated, the meeting shall also decide upon the name of the proposed corporation, the number of the trustees thereof, which shall be, three, six, or nine, and the date, not more than fifteen months thereafter, on which the first annual election of the trustees thereof shall be held; and it may, by a two-thirds vote, decide that all members of the unincorporated church, of full age, in good and regular standing, who have statedly worshiped with such church, but who have not contributed to the financial support thereof, shall also be qualified voters at such meeting, and that such church members, who, for one year next preceding any subsequent corporate meeting, shall have statedly worshiped with such church and have been members thereof in good and regular standing, but have not regularly contributed to the financial support thereof, shall be qualified voters at such corporate meetings. Such meetings shall thereupon elect by ballot from the persons qualified to vote thereat one-third of the number of trustees so decided on, who shall hold office until the first annual election of trustees thereafter, and one-third of such number of trustees who shall hold office until the second annual election of trustees thereafter, one-third of such number of trustees who shall hold office until the third annual election of trustees thereafter, or until the respective successors of such trustees shall be elected. Such meeting shall also elect by ballot a clerk of the corporation, who shall hold his office until the close of the next annual meeting.

The certificate of incorporation.—If the meeting shall decide that such unincorporated church shall become incorporated, the presiding officer of such meeting and the two inspectors of election shall execute a certificate setting forth the name of the proposed corporation, the number of trustees thereof, the names of the persons elected as trustees, the terms of office for which they were respectively elected, and the county or town, city or village, in which its principal place of worship is, or is intended to be, located. On the filing and recording of such certificate, after it shall have been acknowledged or proved as hereinbefore provided, the persons qualified to vote at such meeting and those persons who shall thereafter, from time to time, be qualified voters at the corporate meetings thereof, shall be a corporation by the name stated in such certificate, and the persons therein stated to be elected as trustees of such church shall be the trustees thereof for the terms for which they were respectively elected, and until their respective successors shall be elected.

Time, place, and notice of corporate meetings.—The annual corporate meeting of every church incorporated under this article shall be held at the time and place fixed by its by-laws, or, if no time and place be so fixed, then at a time and place to be first fixed by its trustees, but to be changed only by a by-law to be adopted at an annual meeting. A special corporate meeting of any such church may be called by the body of trustees thereof, on its own motion, and shall be called on the written request of at least ten qualified voters of such church. The trustees shall cause notice of the time and place of its annual corporate meeting, and of the names of any trustees whose successors are to be elected thereat, and if a special meeting, of the business to be transacted thereat, to be publicly read by the minister of such church or any of the trustees thereof at a regular meeting of the church for public worship, on the two successive Sundays immediately preceding such meeting.

Organization and conduct of corporate meetings; qualification of voters. — At every corporate meeting of a church incorporated under this article all persons of full age who, for one year next preceding such meeting, have statedly worshiped with such church and have regularly contributed to its financial support, according to its usages, and no others, shall be qualified voters; but, if so decided, by a two-thirds vote at the original meeting or at any annual corporate meeting thereof after notice of intention so to do has been given with every notice of such meeting, all members of such church of full age and in good and regular standing, by admission into full communion or membership therewith, who have statedly worshiped with such church for one year next preceding the meeting at which they vote, may also be admitted as qualified voters at corporate meetings. At such corporate meetings, the presence of at least six persons qualified to vote thereat shall be necessary to constitute a quorum; and all matters or questions shall be decided by a majority of the qualified voters voting thereon, except that by-laws can be adopted and amended by a two-thirds vote. The clerk of the corporation shall call the meeting to order; and under his supervision the qualified voters then present shall choose a presiding officer and two inspectors of election to receive the ballots cast. The presiding officer and the inspectors of election shall declare the results of the ballots cast on any matter, and shall be the judges of the qualifications of voters. At each annual corporate meeting, successors to those trustees, whose terms of office then expire, shall be elected by ballot from the qualified voters, for a term of three years thereafter, and until their successors shall be elected. A clerk of the corporation shall be elected by ballot, who shall hold office until the close of the next annual meeting, and until his successor shall be elected.

Changing date of annual corporate meetings.—An annual corporate meeting of any church incorporated under this article may change the date of its subsequent annual meetings. If the date fixed for the annual meeting shall be less than six months after the annual meeting at which such change is made, the next annual meeting shall be held one year from the date so fixed. For the purpose of determining the terms of office of trustees, the time between the annual meeting at which such change is made and the next annual meeting thereafter shall be reckoned as one year.

Changing the number of trustees.—Any such incorporated church may, at an annual corporate meeting, change the number of its trustees to three, six, or nine,

classifying them so that the terms of one-third expire
each year, provided that notice of such intended change
be included in the notice of such annual corporate meeting. No such change shall affect the terms of the trustees then in office; and if the change reduces the number
of trustees, elections shall not be held to fill the vacancies
caused by the expiration of the terms of trustees, until
the number of trustees equals the number to which the
trustees are reduced. Whenever the number of trustees
in office is less than the number so determined on, sufficient additional trustees shall be elected to make the
number of trustees equal to the number so determined
on. The trustees so elected, up to and including the one-
third of the number so determined on, shall be elected
for three years, the remainder up to and including one-
third of the number so determined on for two years, and
the remainder for one year.

Meetings of trustees.—Meetings of the trustees of any
such incorporated church shall be called by giving at
least twenty-four hours' notice thereof personally or by
mail to all the trustees; and such notice may be given
by two of the trustees; but by the unanimous consent
of the trustees, a meeting may be held without previous
notice thereof. A majority of the whole number of trustees shall constitute a quorum for the transaction of business, at any meeting lawfully convened.

**The creation and filling of vacancies among trustees of
such churches.**—If any trustee of any such incorporated
church declines to act, resigns, or dies, or ceases to be a
qualified voter at a corporate meeting thereof, his office
shall be vacant; and such vacancy may be filled by the
remaining trustees until the next annual corporate meeting of such church; at which meeting the vacancy shall
be filled for the unexpired term.

Limitation of powers of trustees—The trustees of any
such incorporated church shall have no power to call, settle, or remove a minister, or to fix his salary, nor without
the consent of a corporate meeting to incur debts, beyond
what is necessary for the administration of the temporal

affairs of the church, and for the care of the property of
the corporation; or to fix or change the time, nature, or
order of the public or social worship of such church.

Election and salary of ministers.—The ministers of any
such church shall be called, settled, or removed, and their
salaries fixed, only by the vote of a majority of the members of such corporation duly qualified to vote at elections present and voting at a meeting of such corporation, specially called for that purpose, in the manner
hereinbefore provided for the call of special meetings;
and any such corporation may, by its by-laws, make the
call, settlement, or removal of its ministers depend upon
the concurrent vote of the unincorporated church, present and voting, at a meeting thereof, called for that purpose and such vote shall be necessary to the call, settlement, or removal of such ministers.

Transfer of property to other corporations.—Any incorporated Congregational church, created by or existing
under the laws of the State of New York, or whose last
place of worship was within the State of New York, is
hereby authorized and empowered, by the concurrent
vote of two-thirds of its qualified voters present and voting therefor, at a meeting regularly called for that purpose, and of two-thirds of all its trustees, to direct the
transfer and conveyance of any of its property, real or
personal, which it now has or may hereafter acquire, to
any religious, charitable, or missionary corporation connected with the Congregational denomination and incorporated by or organized under any law or laws of the
State of New York, either solely, or among other purposes, to establish or maintain, or to assist in establishing
or maintaining churches, schools, or mission stations, or
to erect or to assist in the erection of such buildings as
may be necessary for any of such purposes, with or without the payment of any money or other consideration
therefor; and upon such concurrent votes being given, the
trustees shall execute such transfer or conveyance; and
upon the same being made, the title to and the ownership
and right of possession of the property so transferred and

conveyed, shall be vested in and conveyed to such grantee; provided, however, that nothing herein contained
shall impair or affect in any way any existing claim upon
or lien against any property so transferred or conveyed,
or any action at law or legal proceeding; and such transfer shall be subject, in respect to the amount of property
the said grantee may take and hold to the restrictions
and limitations of all laws then in force.   Chapter 621,
Laws 1897.

EVANGELICAL LUTHERAN CHURCHES.

The provisions of article five, chapter seven hundred and twenty-three of the laws of eighteen hundred and ninety-five (general provisions), are applicable to an Evangelical Lutheran Church incorporated before October first, eighteen hundred and ninety-five, if the trustees thereof were then elective as such, and so long as they continue to be elective as such. The special provisions for the incorporation and government of Lutheran churches, article four of chapter seven hundred and twenty-three of the laws of eighteen hundred and twenty-five, are applicable to an Evangelical Lutheran Church incorporated before October first, eighteen hundred and ninety-five, if its trustees were not then elective as such, and so long as its trustees continue not to be elective as such. Chap. 621, Laws 1897.

Decision by Lutheran Churches as to system of incorporation and government.—A meeting for the purpose of incorporating an unincorporated Evangelical Lutheran Church must be called and held in pursuance of the general provisions of chapter seven hundred and twenty-three of the laws of eighteen hundred and ninety-five, except that the first business of such meeting after its organization shall be to determine where such church shall be incorporated and governed in pursuance of the special provisions for the incorporation and government of Lutheran churches or in pursuance of the general provisions. If such meeting determines that such church shall be incorporated and governed in pursuance of the special provisions, then no further proceedings shall be taken in pursuance of the general provisions, and such church may be incorporated and shall be governed after its incorporation in pursuance of the special provisions, except such provisions as are applicable only to churches of a different denomination; and the certificate of incorporation shall recite such determination of such meeting. If such meeting determine that such church shall be incorporated in pursuance of the general provisions, then

this act shall not be applicable thereto, but such church
may be incorporated and shall be governed after incorporation in pursuance of the general provisions. Chap.
35, Laws 1896.

FREE CHURCHES.

How incorporated.—Any seven or more persons of full age, citizens of the United States, and a majority of them being residents of this State, who shall associate themselves for the purpose of founding and continuing one or more free churches, may make, sign and acknowledge, before any officer authorized to take the acknowledgment of deeds of land to be recorded in this State, and may file in the office of the Secretary of State, and also of the Clerk of the County in which any such church is to be established, a certificate in writing, in which shall be stated the name or title by which such society shall be known in the law, the purpose of its organization, and the names of seven trustees, of whom not less than five shall be persons who are not ministers of the Gospel or priests of any denomination, to manage the same; but such certificate shall not be filed, unless with the written consent and approbation of a justice of the supreme court of the district in which any such church shall be intended to be established, or in the city of New York of a judge of the superior court of said city, to be indorsed on such certificate.

Powers, limitations upon property, liability of trustees.—Upon the filing of such certificate the persons named therein as trustees and their their successors, being citizens of the United States and residents of this State, shall be a body politic and corporate, with all the rights, powers, and duties, and subject to all restrictions and obligations and other provisions, so far as the same may be applicable and consistent with this act, specified and contained in the act entitled " An act for the incorporation of benevolent, charitable, scientific, and missionary societies," passed April 12, 1848, and the act amending the same. passed April 7, 1849, except that the limitation in the first of the said acts of the value of the real estate that may be held by any society in the city and county of New York, incorporated under this act, shall not be applicable to any church edifice erected or owned

by such society, or the lot of ground on which the same
may be built; and except that the provision in the first of
the said acts, in relation to the personal liability of trustees, shall be applicable only to the trustees who shall
have consented to the creation of any debt.

Vacancies in boards.—Any vacancies occurring in the
said board of trustees shall be supplied by the remaining
trustees at any legal meeting of the members; but there
shall always be at least, five members of the board who
are not ministers of the gospel or priests of any denomination.

Pews to be free.—The seats or pews in every church
building or edifice owned or occupied by a corporation
organized under this act, shall be forever free for the occupation and use, during public worship, of all persons
choosing to occupy the same, and conducting themselves
with propriety, and no rent, charge, or exaction shall ever
be made or demanded for such occupation or use; nor
shall any real estate belonging to any such corporation
be sold or mortgaged by the trustees thereof, unless by
the direction of the supreme court, to be given in the same
manner and in the like cases as provided by law in relation to religious corporations.—Chap. 218, Laws 1854.

The trustees of a free church may direct where persons
shall sit, and unless one has acquired, by usage or otherwise, some right to a particular seat, a trustee may, after
request and refusal, remove him forcibly therefrom; the
trustee's authority to do so need not be conferred by for-
mal vote at a regular meeting of the board, but it is sufficient if they ratify his action. So held in an action for
damages for ejecting plaintiff. Sheldon *vs.* Vail, 28 Hun.,
354, 1882.

Corporations for acquiring parsonages for presiding elders and camp-meeting grounds.—The presiding elder and a majority of the district stewards residing within a presiding elder's district, erected by an annual conference of the Methodist Episcopal denomination, may become incorporated for the purpose of acquiring, maintaining, and improving real property to be used either as a parsonage for the presiding elder of such district or as a camp ground for camp-meeting purposes, or for both of such objects, by executing, acknowledging, and filing a certificate stating the name and object of the corporation to be formed, the name of such annual conference, and of such presiding elder's district, the names, residences, and official relation to such district of the signers thereof, the number of trustees of such corporation, which shall be three or some multiple of three, not more than twenty-one, the names of such trustees, designating one-third to hold office for three years, one-third to hold office for two years, and one-third to hold office for one year. On filing such certificate the presiding elder and all the stewards of such district, by virtue of their respective offices, shall be a corporation by the name and for the purposes therein stated, and the persons therein named shall be the first trustees thereof. The presiding elder and the stewards of another adjoining presiding elder's district, in this or any other State, may become members of any such corporation, at the time of its formation or any time thereafter, with the consent of such corporation, which has for its sole object, or for one of its objects, the acquiring, maintaining, and improving of real property as a camp ground for camp-meeting purposes, if such presiding elder and a majority of such stewards sign, acknowledge, and cause to be filed in the office of the Secretary of State a certificate stating such object, the name of such district, and the names, residences, and official relations to such district of the signers thereof, with the consent of the original corporation indorsed thereon.

If such a corporation, which has for its sole object or one of its objects, the acquisition and maintenance of camp grounds for camp-meeting purposes, is composed of the presiding elders and the district stewards of more than one presiding elder's district, the number of such trustees shall be apportioned equally, as near as may be, between the different districts, and the presiding elder and district stewards of such district shall elect the names of trustees so apportioned to such district, and the remainder, if any, over an equal division of the trustees, shall be elected by all the members of the corporation.

A person holding property in trust for the purposes of a parsonage for the presiding elder of a district, and his successors in office, or for camp meeting purposes, for the Methodist Episcopal denomination, may convey the same to a corporation formed for the purpose of acquiring such property within the district in which the property is situated. Meetings held under the direction of such a corporation upon camp grounds owned by it shall be deemed religious meetings, within the provision of law relating to disturbances of religious meetings, and the trustees of such a corporation shall have the powers of peace officers with relation thereto. Whenever such a corporation or any camp-ground association owns land bordering upon any navigable waters, to be used for any camp-meeting purposes only, such corporation or association may regulate or prohibit the landing of persons or vessels at the wharves, piers, or shores upon such grounds during the holding of religious services thereon.

If the trustees of any such corporation heretofore incorporated have not been classified, so that the terms of office of one-third of their number expire each year, the trustees of such corporation shall be elected annually by the members thereof; but if the trustees of any such corporation have been so classified, one-third of the total number of trustees shall be elected annually to hold office for three years. Such a corporation heretofore incorporated may, by a majority vote, at an annual meeting, or at a special meeting duly called therefor, determine to change the number of its trustees to three, or some multiple thereof—not more than twenty-one. On such determination a majority of the trustees shall sign, acknowledge, and file in the offices where the original certificate of such corporation is filed, a supplemental certificate, specifying such reduction or increase; and thereon the number of trustees shall be the number stated in such certificate. If the number of trustees is increased, the corporation shall elect, at its next annual meeting, a sufficient number of trustees to hold office for one, two, or three years respectively, so that the terms of office of one-third of the whole number of trustees of such corporation shall expire at each annual meeting thereafter.

If the number is reduced, the corporation shall thereafter elect at its annual meetings one-third of the number of trustees specified in such supplemental certificate, but the trustees in office when such certificate is filed shall continue in office until the expiration of their terms, respectively. Chap. 723, Laws 1895.

The meeting for incorporation.—Notice of a meeting for the purpose of incorporating an unincorporated Protestant Episcopal parish or congregation, and of electing the first church wardens and vestrymen thereof, shall specify the object, time, and place of such meeting, and shall be made public for at least two weeks prior to such meeting, either by open reading of such notice in time of divine service, at the usual place of worship of such parish or congregation, or by posting the same conspicuously on the outer door of such place of worship. Only men of full age who have been regular attendants at the worship of such parish or congregation and contributors to the support thereof for one year next prior to such meeting, or since the establishment of such parish or congregation, shall be qualified to vote at such meeting. The action of the meeting upon any matter or question shall be decided by a majority of the qualified voters voting thereon, a quorum being present.

The officiating minister, or if there be none, or he shall be necessarily absent, any other person qualified to vote at the meeting, who is called to the chair, shall preside thereat. Such presiding officer shall receive the votes, be the judge of the qualification of voters, and declare the result of the votes cast at such meeting. The polls of the meeting shall remain open for one hour or longer, in the discretion of the presiding officer, or, if required, by a vote of the majority of the voters present. The meeting shall decide whether such unincorporated parish or congregation shall become incorporated. If such decision be in favor of incorporation, such meeting shall decide upon the name of the proposed incorporation; what secular day of the week, beginning with the first Sunday in Advent, shall be the date of the regular annual election; whether the vestrymen thereof shall be three, six, or nine; and shall be elected by ballot from the persons qualified to be voters thereat, who have been baptized; one-third of the number of vestrymen so decided upon to hold office until the first annual election, to be held thereafter, one-third of such number to hold office until one year after such annual election, and one-third of such number to hold office until two years after such annual election; and shall elect from such qualified voters who are communicants in the Protestant Episcopal Church, two persons to be church wardens thereof, one to hold office until such annual election, and one to hold office until one year after such annual election. Chap. 358, Laws, 1898.

The certificate of incorporation. — If such meeting shall decide in favor of incorporation and comply with the next preceding section, the presiding officer of such meeting, and at least two other persons present and voting thereat, shall execute and acknowledge a certificate of incorporation, setting forth:

1. The fact of the calling and holding of such meeting.

2. The name of the corporation, as decided upon thereat.

3. The county and the town, city, or village, in which its principal place of worship is, or is intended to be located.

4. The day of the week, commencing with the first Sunday in Advent, upon which the annual election shall be held.

5. The number of vestrymen decided upon at such meeting.

6. The names of the vestrymen elected at such meeting and the term of office of each.

7. The names of the church wardens elected at such meeting and the term of office of each.

On filing such certificate in the office of the clerk of the county, so specified therein, the church wardens and vestrymen so elected, and their successors in office, together with the rector, when there is one, shall form a vestry, and shall be the trustees of such church or congregation; and they and their successors shall thereupon, by virtue of this act, be a body corporate, by the name or title expressed in such certificate, and shall have power, from time to time, to adopt by-laws for its governance. Such corporation shall be an incorporated church, and may be termed also an incorporated parish.

Corporate trustees, vestry; powers and duties thereof.—No meeting of the vestry or trustees of any incorporated Protestant Episcopal parish or church shall be held unless either all the members thereof are present, or three days' notice thereof shall be given to each member thereof, by the rector, in writing, either personally or by mail, or, if there be no rector, or if he be incapable of acting, by one of the church wardens; except that twenty-four hours' notice of the first meeting of the vestry or trustees after an annual election shall be sufficient, provided such meeting shall be held within three days after the election. To constitute a quorum of the vestry or board of trustees there must be present either:

1. The rector, at least one of the church wardens, and a majority of the vestrymen; or,

2. The rector, both church wardens and one less than a majority of the vestrymen; or,

3. If the rector be absent from the diocese and shall have been so absent for over four calendar months, or if the meeting be called by the rector and he be absent therefrom, or be incapable of acting, one church warden and a majority of the vestrymen, or both church wardens and one less than a majority of the vestrymen.

But if there be a rector of the parish, no measure shall be taken, in his absence, in any case, for effecting the sale or disposition of the real property of the corporation, nor for the sale or disposition of the capital or principal of the personal property of the corporation, nor shall any act be done which shall impair the rights of such rector. The presiding officer of the vestry or trustees shall be the rector, or, if there be none, or he be absent, the church warden who shall be called to the chair by a majority of the votes, if both the church wardens be present; or the church warden present, if but one be present. At each meeting of the vestry or trustees each member thereof shall be entitled to one vote. The vestry shall have power to fill a vacancy occurring in the office of a church warden or vestryman by death, resignation, or otherwise than by expiration of term, until the next annual election, at which, if such vacancy would continue thereafter, it shall be filled for the remainder of the unexpired term. The vestry may, subject to the canons of the Protestant Episcopal Church in the United States, and of the diocese in which the parish or church is situated, by a majority vote, elect a rector to fill a vacancy occurring in the rectorship of the parish, and may fix the salary or compensation of the rector.

Annual elections of incorporated Protestant Episcopal parishes. — The annual election of a Protestant Episcopal parish, hereafter incorporated, shall be held on the secular day in the week commencing with the first Sunday in Advent, designated in its certificate of incorporation. The annual election of an incorporated Protestant Episcopal parish or church heretofore incorporated shall be held on the day fixed for such annual election, by or in pursuance of law, or if no such date be so fixed, then on the Monday next after the first Sunday in Advent. Notice of such annual election shall be read by the rector of the parish, or if there be none, or he be absent, by the officiating minister or by a church warden thereof, on each of the two Sundays next preceding such election, in the time of divine service, or if, for any reason, the usual place of worship of the parish be not open for divine service, the notice shall be posted conspicuously on the outer door of the place of worship for two weeks next preceding the election. Such notice shall specify the place, day, and hour of holding the election, the name and term of office of each church warden and vestryman whose term of office shall then expire, or whose office shall then be vacant for any cause, and the office for which each such officer is to be then elected. The meeting for such annual election shall be held immediately after morning service. The presiding officer of such meeting shall be the rector thereof, if there be one, or if there be none, or he be absent, one of the church wardens elected for the purpose, by a majority of the duly qualified voters present, or if no church warden be present, a vestryman elected in like manner.

Such presiding officer shall be the judge of the qualification of the voters, shall receive the votes cast, and shall declare the result of the votes cast at such election. The presiding officer of such meeting shall enter the proceedings of the meeting in the book of the minutes of the vestry, sign his name thereto, and offer the same to as many qualified voters present, as he shall think fit, to be also signed by them. Only men of full age, belonging to the parish, who have been regular attendants at its worship and contributors to its support for at least twelve months prior to such election, or since the establishment of such parish, shall be qualified voters at any such election. The action of the meeting upon any matter or question shall be decided by a majority of the qualified voters voting thereon. The polls of the election shall continue open for one hour, and longer, in the discretion of the presiding officer, or, if required, by a vote of the majority of the qualified voters present and voting. The church wardens and vestrymen shall be elected by ballot from persons qualified to vote at such election, and no person shall be eligible for election as church warden, unless he be also a communicant in the Protestant Episcopal Church, nor be eligible for election as vestryman, unless he shall have been baptized. At each annual election of an incorporated Protestant Episcopal parish hereafter incorporated, one church warden shall be elected to hold office for two years; and one-third of the total number of the vestrymen of the parish shall be elected to hold office for three years. At each annual election of an incorporated Protestant Episcopal parish or church heretofore incorporated two church wardens and the total number of its vestrymen shall be elected to hold office for one year thereafter, unless the terms of office of but one church warden or of but one-third of its vestrymen shall then expire, in which case one church warden shall be elected to hold office for two years, and one-third of the total number of its vestrymen shall be elected to hold office for three years. Each church warden and vestryman shall hold office after the expiration of his term, until his successor shall be chosen.

Changing the number of vestrymen of Protestant Episcopal parishes hereafter incorporated.—If the vestry of a Protestant Episcopal parish, hereafter incorporated, shall, by resolution, recommend that, the number of vestrymen of such parish be changed to either three, six, or nine vestrymen, notice of such recommendation shall be included in the notice of the next annual election of such parish, and be submitted to the meeting. If such recommendation be ratified by such meeting, the presiding officer thereof, and at least two qualified voters present thereat, shall execute and acknowledge a certificate, setting forth such resolution of the vestry; the fact that notice thereof had been given with the notice of such annual election; that the meeting had ratified the same; and the number of vestrymen so decided on. Such certificate shall be filed in the office of the clerk of the county in which the original certificate of incorporation is filed and recorded, and such change in the number of vestrymen shall take effect at the time of the next annual election thereafter. If the number of vestrymen be thereby increased, then, in addition to the number of vestrymen to be elected at such annual election, one-third of such increased number of vestrymen shall be elected to hold office for one year thereafter, one-third of such increased number shall be elected to hold office for two years thereafter, and one-third of such increased number shall be elected to hold office for three years thereafter. If the number of vestrymen by such change be reduced, such reduction shall not affect the term of office of any vestryman duly elected, and at such next annual election, and at each annual election thereafter, one-third of such reduced number of vestrymen shall be elected to hold office for three years.

Changing date of annual election, number and term of office of church wardens in Protestant Episcopal Churches heretofore incorporated. — If the vestry of a Protestant Episcopal parish heretofore incorporated, shall, by resolution, recommend that the date of the annual election be changed to a secular day in the week beginning with the first Sunday in Advent, or that the number of vestrymen be changed to three, six, or nine, and that the terms of office of the church wardens be changed so that one warden shall be elected annually, notice of such recommendation or recommendations shall be included in the notice of the next annual election of such parish, and be submitted to the meeting. If such recommendation or recommendations be ratified by such meeting, the presiding officer thereof, and at least two qualified voters present thereat, shall execute and acknowledge a certificate setting forth such resolution of the vestry; the fact that notice thereof had been given with the notice of the annual meeting; that such meeting had ratified the same; the date determined upon for the annual election of the parish; the number of vestrymen so decided on; and the fact that the meeting determined to thereafter elect church wardens, so that the term of one warden shall expire annually. Such certificate shall be filed in the office of the clerk of the county in which the original certificate of incorporation is filed and recorded. If the meeting determined to change the date of the annual election, the next annual election shall be held on the day in the week beginning with the first Sunday in Advent, determined on by such meeting, and the terms of the vestrymen and church wardens which, pursuant to law, would expire at the next annual election, shall expire and their successors shall be elected on such day. If the meeting determine to change the number of vestrymen and manner of electing wardens and vestrymen, there shall be elected at the first annual election thereafter, one-third of the number of vestrymen so determined on, to hold office for three years; one-third thereof to hold office for two years, and one-third thereof to hold

office for one year; and one church warden to hold office
for one year, and one to hold office for two years; and
thereafter, at the annual election, there shall be elected
one-third of the number of vestrymen determined on at
such meeting, and one church warden.

**Changing the qualifications of voters and the qualifi-
cations of wardens and vestrymen.**—If the vestry of a
Protestant Episcopal parish heretofore incorporated shall
by resolution recommend that the qualifications of voters
and the qualifications of wardens and vestrymen be
changed to conform in both cases to the requirements
of section thirty-three of this statute, notice of such recommendation or recommendations shall be included in
the notice of the next annual election of such parish, and
be submitted to the meeting. If such recommendation
or recommendations be ratified by such meeting, the presiding officer thereof and at least two qualified voters
present thereat, shall execute and acknowledge a certificate setting forth such resolution of the vestry, the fact
that notice thereof had been given with the notice of such
annual election, and that the meeting had ratified the
same. Such certificate shall be filed in the office of the
clerk of the county in which the original certificate of incorporation is filed and recorded. Chap. 358. Laws of
1898. Approved April 20.

REFORMED DUTCH, PRESBYTERIAN, REFORMED PRESBYTERIAN, AND EVANGELICAL LUTHERAN CHURCHES.

The title of article four of chapter seven hundred and twenty-three of the laws of eighteen hundred and ninety-five (entitled, "An act in relation to religious corporations, constituting chapter forty-two of the general laws," is hereby amended to read as follows: Special provisions for the incorporation and government of Reformed Dutch, Presbyterian, Reformed Presbyterian, and Lutheran Churches.

Section 61 of such law is hereby amended to read as follows:

Decision by Lutheran and Presbyterian churches as to the system of incorporation and government.—A meeting for the purpose of incorporating an unincorporated Evangelical Lutheran Church or an unincorporated Presbyterian church in connection with the Presbyterian church in the United States of America, must be called and held in pursuance of the provisions of the next article of this chapter, except that the first business of such meeting after its organization shall be to determine whether such church shall be incorporated and governed in pursuance of this article, or in pursuance of the next article of this chapter. If such meeting determines that such church shall be incorporated and governed in pursuance of this article, then no further proceeding shall be taken in pursuance of the next article, and such church may be incorporated and shall be governed after its incorporation in pursuance of the provisions of the following sections of this article, except such provisions as are applicable only to churches of a different denomination; and the certificate of incorporation shall recite such determination of such meeting. If such church is an unincorporated Presbyterian church in connection with the Presbyterian church in the United States of America, and such meeting determine that it shall be incorporated and governed in pursuance of this article, then the meeting

shall also determine whether by virtue of their office the
deacons only of such church, or the pastor, elders, and
deacons of such church, or the pastors and elders of such
church, shall be the trustees of such corporation; and the
certificate of the incorporation shall recite such determination of such meeting. If such meeting determine
that such church shall be incorporated and governed in
pursuance of the next article of this chapter, then this
article shall not be applicable thereto, but such church
may be incorporated, and shall be governed after its incorporation in pursuance of the provisions of the next article of this chapter, except such provisions as are applicable to churches of a single religious denomination only.
—Chap. 190, Laws 1896.

Section 62, Chap. 723, laws 1895, is amended so as to
read as follows:

**Incorporation of Reformed Dutch, Presbyterian, Re-
formed Presbyterian, and Evangelical Lutheran churches
under this article.**—If an unincorporated church in connection with the Reformed Church in America, the true
Reformed Dutch Church in the United States of America,
the Reformed Presbyterian Church, or with the Evangelical Lutheran Church, determine to incorporate in pursuance of this article, the minister or ministers and elders
and deacons thereof, or if a Presbyterian church in connection with the Presbyterian church in the United States
of America, the officers determined upon as the trustees
thereof by the meeting for incorporation, or such of them
as may be in office, shall execute, acknowledge, and cause
to be filed and recorded, a certificate in pursuance of this
article. The deacons of a Reformed Presbyterian church
may alone sign such certificate if authorized so to do by
such church. Such certificate of incorporation shall state
the name of the proposed corporation, the county and
town, city, or village, where its principal place of worship
is or is intended to be located, and, if it be an Evangelical
Lutheran church, or a Presbyterian church in connection
with the Presbyterian Church in the United States of
America, the fact that a meeting of such church, duly

called, decided that it be incorporated under this article. If it be signed by the deacons of a Reformed Presbyterian church, it shall state that they were authorized so to do by such church. If it be the certificate of a Presbyterian church in connection with the Presbyterian church in the United States of America, it shall recite that the officers signing such certificate were determined upon by the meeting for incorporation to be the trustees of such corporation. On filing such certificate such church shall be a corporation by the name stated therein, and the minister or ministers, if any, and the elders and deacons of such church shall, by virtue of their offices, be the trustees of such corporation, except that if it be a Reformed Presbyterian church, the certificate of incorporation of which shall have been, in pursuance of law, signed by its deacons only, the deacons of such church shall, by virtue of their offices, be the trustees of such corporation; and except that if it be a Presbyterian church in connection with the Presbyterian Church in the United States of America, the officers determined upon by the meeting for incorporation shall, by virtue of their offices, be the trustees of such corporation.—Chap. 190, Laws 1896.

Section 66, Chap. 723, laws 1895, is amended to read as follows:

Evangelical Lutheran and Presbyterian churches, changing system of electing trustees.—If the trustees of an incorporated Evangelical Lutheran church, or an incorporated Presbyterian church in connection with the Presbyterian Church in the United States of America, shall at any time be elective in pursuance of the next article of this chapter, the church may, at an annual corporate meeting, if notice thereof be given with the notice of such meeting, determine, if an Evangelical Lutheran church, that the minister or ministers and elders and deacons thereof, or the pastor and elders thereof, shall thereafter constitute the trustees thereof, and thereon the trustees of such church shall sign, acknowledge and cause to be filed and recorded, a certificate stating the fact of such determination, and if an Evangelical Lutheran church, that the minister or ministers and elders and deacons thereof, or the pastor and the elders and deacons thereof, or the pastor and elders thereof, shall thereafter constitute the trustees thereof, and thereon the trustees of such church shall sign, acknowledge, and cause to be filled and recorded a certificate stating the fact of such determination, and if an Evangelical Lutheran church, the names of the minister or ministers, if any, and of the elders and deacons of such church, or, if a Presbyterian church in connection with the Presbyterian Church in the United States of America, the names of the officers determined upon to be the ex-officio trustees therof; and thereon the terms of office of such elective trustees shall cease, and the minister or ministers and the elders and deacons of such church, if an Evangelical Lutheran church, or the officers determined upon by such corporate meeting; if a Presbyterian church in connection with the Presbyterian Church in the United States of America, and their successors in office shall, by virtue of their respective offices, be the trustees of such church. If at any time the officers of an incorporated Evangelical Lutheran church, or an incorporated Presbyterian church in connection with the Presbyterian Church in the United States of America, which officers, by virtue of the offices, constitute the trustees thereof, shall determine to submit to a meeting of such church corporation the question whether the trustees of such church shall be thereafter elective in pursuance of the next article of this chapter, they shall cause a corporate meeting of such church to be called and held in the manner provided by sections eighty-four and eighty-five of chapter seven hundred and twenty-three of the laws of eighteen hundred and ninety-five, and also whether the number of trustees shall be three, six, or nine, and the date of the annual corporate meeting of the church. If such meeting shall determine that such trustees shall thereafter be elective, the presiding officer thereof and at least two other persons present and voting thereat, shall sign, acknowledge, and cause to be filed and recorded in the office of the clerk of the county

in which the certificate of incorporation of such church is
filed, a certificate of such determination of such meeting;
and thereafter the trustees of such church shall be elective in pursuance of the next article of this chapter. At
the next annual corporate meeting after the filing of such
certificate, one-third of the number of trustees so determined on shall be elected to hold office for one year, one-
third for two years, and one-third for three years, and the
officers of such church shall then cease to be such trustees, and thereafter article five of chapter seven hundred
and twenty-three of the laws of eighteen hundred and
ninety-five shall apply to such church. At each subsequent annual corporate meeting of such church, one-third
of the number of trustees so determined on shall be
elected to hold office for three years.—Chap. 190, Laws
1896.

Incorporation of Roman Catholic and Greek Churches.
—An unincorporated Roman Catholic church, or an unincorporated Christian Orthodox Catholic church of the Eastern Confession, in this State may become incorporated as a church by executing, acknowledging and filing a certificate of incorporation, stating the corporate name by which such church shall be known, and the county, town, city, or village where its principal place of worship is, or is intended to be located.

A certificate of incorporation of an unincorporated Roman Catholic church shall be executed and acknowledged by the Roman Catholic Archbishop or Bishop, and the Vicar-General of the diocese in which its place of worship is, and by the rector of the church, and by two laymen, members of such church, who shall be selected by such officials, or by a majority of such officials.

A certificate of incorporation of an unincorporated Christian Orthodox Catholic church of the Eastern Confession shall be executed and acknowledged by the Envoy-Extraordinary and Minister Plenipotentiary, and the Consul-General of Russia to the United States, then acknowledged and received as such by the United States.

On filing such certificate such church shall be a corporation by the name stated in the certificate.

Government of incorporated Roman Catholic and Greek Churches. —The Archbishop or Bishop and the Vicar-General of the diocese to which any incorporated Roman Catholic church belongs, the rector of such church, and their successors in office, shall, by virtue of their offices, be trustees of such church. Two laymen, members of such incorporated church, selected by such officers or a majority of them, shall also be trustees of such incorporated church, and such officers and such laymen trustees shall together constitute the board of trustees thereof. The two laymen signing the certificate of incorporation of an unincorporated Roman Catholic church shall be the two laymen trustees thereof during the first year

of its corporate existence. The term of office of the two
laymen trustees of an incorporated Roman Catholic
church shall be one year. Whenever the office of any
such layman trustee shall become vacant by expiration
of term of office or otherwise, his successor shall be appointed from members of the church, by such officers or
a majority of them. No act or proceeding of the trustees
of any such incorporated church shall be valid without
the sanction of the Archbishop or Bishop of the diocese
to which such church belongs, or in case of their absence
or inability to act, without the sanction of the Vicar-General or of the administrator of such diocese.

The Envoy-Extraordinary and Minister Plenipotentiary
and the Consul-General of Russia to the United States
acknowledged and received as such, and their successors
in office shall, by virtue of office, be the trustees of every
incorporated Christian Orthodox Catholic church of the
Eastern Confession in this State. The trustees of any
such church shall have the power to fix and change the
salary of the rector and his assistant, appointed or com-
missioned according to the rules and usages of the denomination to which such church belongs.—Chap. 723,
Laws 1895.

Trusts for Shakers and Friends.—All deeds or declarations of trust of real or personal property, executed and delivered before January first, eighteen hundred and thirty, or since May fifth, eighteen hundred and thirty-nine, to any person in trust for any united society of Shakers, or heretofore executed and delivered, shall be vested in three trustees the legal estates and religious society of Friends, shall be valid. Trusts of real and personal property, for the benefit and use of the members of any united society of Shakers, or of any meeting of the religious society of Friends, may hereafter be created, according to the religious constitution of such society of Shakers, or the regulations and rules of discipline of such society of Friends. Such deeds or declarations of trust, heretofore or hereafter executed and delivered, shall vest in the trustees the legal estates and interests purported to be conveyed or declared thereby, to and for the uses and purposes declared therein; and such legal estates and trusts, and all legal authority with which the original trustees were vested by virtue of their appointment and conferred powers, shall descend to their successors in office or trust, who may be chosen in conformity to the constitution of such society, or the direction of such meeting. This section does not impair or diminish the rights of any person, meeting, or association claiming to be a meeting, had to any real or personal property held in trust for the use and benefit of any meeting of such society, before the division of such society which took place at the annual meeting held in the city of New York in May, eighteen hundred and twenty-eight. No society of Shakers, or meeting of Friends, shall become beneficially interested in real or personal property, the clear annual value or income of which exceeds twenty-five thousand dollars. No person shall be a trustee at the same time of more than one society of Shakers or meeting of Friends. A society of Shakers includes all persons of the religious belief of the people called Shakers, resident within the same county. Chap. 723, Laws 1895.

Conveyance of trust property of friends.—The trustee or trustees, or the survivor of any trustees, of any meeting of the religious Society of Friends, appointed pursuant to the last preceding section, may sell, convey, and grant or demise any or all of the trust property described in said trust deed or declaration of trust. to any person absolutely or in trust for such meeting, whenever any meeting of said society by resolution so directs. Any conveyance of real estate or property so held in trust by a meeting of the religious Society of Friends. which is hereafter made in pursuance of a resolution of such meeting as provided herein, shall be as valid and effectual for the conveyance of the title of any real estate so held in trust as if the heirs of any trustee who has died prior to the passage of such resolution had joined in the execution of such conveyance or demise. Any instrument for the sale or demise of such property shall embody such resolution, and be executed by such trustee or trustees; and in such acknowledgment such trustee or trustees shall make an affidavit that the person or persons executing such conveyance or demise are the trustee or trustees of the trust property, and that the resolution embodied in such conveyance or demise was duly passed by such meeting. Such affidavit shall be prima facie evidence of the facts therein stated. Chap. 723, Laws 1895.

Incorporation of a union church.—Two or more unincorporated churches, which separately agree on a plan of union and determine to meet together for the purpose of being incorporated as a union church, may be incorporated as a union church in pursuance of the preceding provisions, and thereafter such union church shall be governed by such provisions as near as may be, except as otherwise provided. A notice of such joint meeting shall be given to the congregation of each church, in pursuance to the preceding provisions relating to notice of meeting for incorporation in every respect, as if it were a notice of a meeting for the separate incorporation of such church under such provisions, except that the notice shall state in substance that a joint meeting of such incorporated churches, which shall be specified in the notice, will be held for the purpose of incorporating such churches as a union church, and electing trustees thereof at a time and place specified in the notice, which place may be the usual place of worship of either of such churches, or any other reasonably convenient place. Such notice must be signed by at least six persons from each of such churches who would be authorized to sign a notice for the meeting of each church, respectively, for the purpose of incorporating it under such provisions.

The preceding provisions shall be applicable to the organization and conduct of such meeting, the matters to be determined upon, and the certificate of incorporation to be executed and filed accordingly, except that the presiding officer of such joint meeting shall be the oldest person present at such meeting who would be entitled to preside at a meeting of either of such churches singly for the purposes of incorporation in pursuance of such provisions. All persons who would be qualified to vote at such meeting of either of such churches held singly shall be qualified voters at such joint meeting, and the number of trustees of the union church after incorporation, to be selected from each such church, may be agreed on by such unincorporated churches, and the trustees shall be selected by each of such churches accordingly.

The certificate of incorporation shall set forth the plan of union agreed on and the number of trustees of the incorporated union church to be selected by each unincorporated church.—Chap. 723. Laws 1895.

Government of incorporated union churches.—Any union church or society having a common place of worship, or holding property belonging jointly to the several societies composing the same, but the sole right of occupancy of which is reserved to each of them in proportion to their interest in such property, or the money originally paid therefor by each, or in accordance with their plan of union agreed on, may, if any one or more of the churches or societies comprising such union church or society has ceased to exist, on the request of such remaining churches or society, redistribute and divide the time of occupancy among such remaining societies in proportion to their contributions to such property respectively, or in accordance with a new plan of union agreed on by them. Such redistribution shall be made by the trustees of said union church or society on written notice to the societies which it is alleged have ceased to exist; but no such society shall be deemed to have ceased to exist unless it has failed or neglected for a period of five consecutive years next preceding such request for redistribution, to hold meetings, and have a clerk or secretary, and keep a list or registry of its members, or to have preaching, prayer. or conference meetings, or other religious services in keeping with the usages of the denomination to which it belongs.

Any one of the societies composing a union church or society which shall have built a church edifice in the same village or neighborhood in which it holds its religious services shall not thereby lose or forfeit in any way any of its rights or privileges in such union society, and the maintaining of divine worship. or contributing to its support in its own building shall be regarded the same as if it held its meetings in the church building of such union societies. Any notice for the election of trustees of the union society or for any other purpose which the law requires to be read or given at the time of divine service, may be read or given in the church edifice so built by any one of such societies, if at the time religious services are not held in the church edifice of such union society. But such notice must be posted on the outer door of such union church edifice at least fifteen days before the meeting. If any society composing any such church union or society has a greater interest in the occupancy of the church building than others, unless the several churches composing the union church or society have agreed otherwise, the number of trustees shall be odd, and the trustees shall be elected from such societies in proportion to their respective interests in the union, church, or society, as nearly as may be. Any society composing such union, church, or society, which has built for itself a church edifice and become incorporated, may sell its interest and right of occupancy in such union society, and convey the same, when authorized so to do by a two-thirds vote of the voters thereof qualified to vote for union trustees, at a special meeting called for that purpose. The proceeds of such sale shall be used for the benefit of its church property. Chap. 723, Laws 1895.

Trustees of a church in connection with the United Brethren in Christ.—If any church connected with the denomination known as the United Brethren in Christ shall neglect or omit to elect trustees at any annual election at which trustees should have been elected, the quarterly conference of the circuit, station, or mission of such denomination may elect such trustees for full terms, or to fill vacancies, in accordance with the rules and usages of such denomination.—Chap. 723, Laws 1895.